Praying Our Stories

Praying Our Stories:
Reflections
for Youth Ministers

by Daniel Ponsetto

Saint Mary's Press
Christian Brothers Publications
Winona, Minnesota

Thank you . . .

Sue, for encouraging me to write this book.

Joey and Julian, for the things you teach me daily, and for the joy of being your dad.

Mom and Dad, for your constant love, and for believing in me.

Cliff Anderson, Ronn Huth, Patty Alfeld, Jack Carpenter, Dean Borgman, Mike and Mary Wilson, Kent McDonald, and Fr. Dick Harrington, for teaching me what you know about youth work, and especially for laughing with me.

Henri Nouwen, for helping me to see how universal our personal experiences really are.

Fr. Bob Stamschror, for trimming the fat off of my original manuscript, and for your patience and good humor.

The publishing team for this book included Robert P. Stamschror, development editor; Barbara Augustyn Sirovatka, manuscript editor and typesetter; McCormick Creative, cover design; Reg Sandland, illustrator; pre-press, printing, and binding by the graphics division of Saint Mary's Press.

The acknowledgments continue on page 103.

Printed in the United States of America
Printing: 6 5 4 3 2 1
Year: 1998 97 96 95 94 93 92
ISBN 0-88489-281-6

*I dedicate this book
to
my wife and friend, Sue.*

Contents

Introduction

My Story, Your Story

My older sister tells me that when I was two years old I bit the legs off her pet turtle. At least, that's the story that gets told, year in and year out, when I am reunited with my family. It is just one of the many childhood tales that are retold whenever my family sits down together for a meal, with each of the different stories gaining new drama and greater detail as the years advance. My memory of the turtle story is that I may have actually bitten one, or possibly two, of the poor creature's legs off, but the current opinion in my family is that I had gotten all four legs and was getting ready to decapitate the beloved pet when I was discovered.

Everybody loves a story. The next time you are listening to a speaker, notice how you respond when he or she begins to tell a personal story. If you are like me, you perk up a notch or two. The power of stories is due to the universal element in them. While the particulars of a personal story may be unique, there is usually enough common experience within the story to enable a personal connection. We nod, laugh, cry, or shake our head at each other's stories because we identify with them. "No, I have never fallen off a cow in Boise . . . but I know exactly what you're talking about!" That is the power of stories.

Some of the most encouraging and valuable times in my years of youth work have been spent sitting with other youth ministers, swapping stories while sipping coffee or beer. I have always taken great comfort in hearing others share their joys, their disappointments, their fears, their laughter, and their tears. And it has been nice to have others listen to my stories with empathy and, on occasion, reassure me that I am not alone in this work; that reassurance has been important for me over the years.

At times in the past few years, I have written in a journal about my daily experiences in youth work. Writing helps me reflect on who I am in ministry, why God has called me to this crazy vocation, and what God is doing in my life as a result of my relationships with young people. I find that the time I spend writing is a great opportunity for sharing my stories with

God and allowing the Holy Spirit to speak to me through these experiences.

My primary place for inspiration happens to be in the shower. It was there one morning that the thought occurred to me: *If I benefit so much from listening to the stories of other youth ministers, is it possible that others in youth work would be encouraged by my stories?* I was struck by the fact that there weren't many devotional or reflective resources for youth workers—the overwhelming emphasis in youth ministry publishing was on programmatic materials. I wondered if volunteer and professional youth workers had an even greater need for resources that would affirm them and help them maintain a perspective on how God was working in their life and in their ministry experiences.

After receiving some enthusiastic encouragement from my wife, Sue, and the support of Fr. Bob Stamschror at Saint Mary's Press, the present book began to take shape.

The Audience

The stories and reflections offered here are intended for people in any kind of youth ministry. In my own mind that is a broad audience: you may be a full-time coordinator in a parish, a volunteer, a confirmation teacher, a priest, a youth pastor, a coach, a director of religious education, a high school math teacher, and so on. Because the experiences I have chosen to reflect on come out of my years both in Young Life and in Catholic youth ministry, I hope that they may appeal to a broad range of persons ministering in diverse contexts and Christian traditions.

Preview

The format for each reflection is simple. First, I share a story from my daily experiences with young people or other youth ministers. The story and reflections are followed by a short meditation taken from the Scriptures or from other spiritual writing. Reflective questions are offered, followed by a prayer.

I have tried to be vulnerable in sharing my stories. This has not always been easy for me because many of them do not present me in the most favorable light.

I have used fictitious names in some of the stories and altered settings for reasons that will be obvious to you as you read. I do not feel that any of these changes harm the integrity or truthfulness of the stories themselves.

My hope rests on the universal quality of the stories, so that even though the particulars of the story are uniquely mine, you will nod, smile, or sigh as you read and identify with some of the situations and issues. But it is the situations and issues that take place in your own ministry—your own stories—that I hope you may reflect on in prayer. My stories are simply a means for you to tap into your own stories and to uncover the workings of God revealed there.

I pray that this book will be a source of encouragement for you in your work with young people and that in praying with it, you will come to a fuller knowledge of how deeply you are loved by God.

Part 1

◆

STRUGGLE

❖ 1 ❖
I Love These Kids:
But Not Tonight!

Today I was in my office keeping busy with nothing in particular: a phone call here, some staff business there, and probably some goofing off in between. As I was going about my work, I suddenly remembered that it was Wednesday, the night I meet with seven young people for Bible study and prayer. This is a great group of kids, and I enjoy spending time with them. We have developed a sense of community, so it is easy and fun to be together. But I experienced a strange and unexpected sinking feeling in the pit of my stomach as I thought about being with the kids.

I was surprised by the sudden feeling of fear, even dread, that came over me as I remembered my meeting. Almost immediately I began to analyze what the feeling meant: *Why is the thought of tonight's meeting producing so much fear and reluctance? Don't I like being with these people?* I thought I did, yet I couldn't deny that sinking feeling as I remembered what night it was.

The meeting has now come and gone. Our time together was fine, nothing out of the ordinary, just our usual good time of focusing some on the Scriptures, praying together a little bit, and enjoying each other's fellowship. Yet I am left wondering why I experienced that sinking feeling earlier in the day. As I think about the episode, I realize that it is not the first time in my years of ministry that I have felt that dread. In fact, if I am honest, I have to say that the experience is not uncommon at all. I have felt it while driving to the high school to watch a practice, while preparing to meet with a volunteer leader, and before leaving for a weekend retreat with young people. I have felt it many times.

So what brings it on? I really do like the kids I was with tonight, yet the thought of being with them produced, for an instant anyway, anxiety and fear. I am not sure if I have the answer to the "pit phenomenon" in my life, but I am going to venture a guess.

I suspect the cause is twofold. First, I think the dread is a product of self-concern. Yes, I like the kids I was with tonight, but I would have been secretly happy if they had all called me today, just this day, to say that they couldn't make the meeting. Then I could have stayed home with my family and quite possibly—without guilt—watched some ridiculous TV sitcom while sprawling on the couch and eating a pint of Ben & Jerry's Reverse Chocolate Chunk ice cream. It would have been like a free holiday when a major snowstorm hits or when the electricity is knocked out by a heavy thunderstorm and everything gets cancelled. Although such happenings can be inconvenient or disappointing, we get some unexpected bonus time to do things like saying hello to our spouse or reading or sleeping. But without a forecast for snow tonight, my concern for my time had no place to hide.

The other cause of anxiety is the pressure I feel to create something good. Having a meeting tonight meant I had to come up with something creative, something meaningful, something edifying for others. My thoughts were panicky: *They're going to expect something from me tonight. I just can't go there and hope that the Spirit will inspire us all in some incredible way. Believe me, I've tried it enough times!* That sinking feeling comes as I realize that I have to prepare something that really is "good." Part of that is healthy: I want my contributions to be good because I want kids to grow closer to the Lord and get excited about their faith. But part of it, I'm sure, is motivated again by my self-concern: I want my contributions to be good so kids will keep coming, so kids will think I am relevant, so kids will, yes, like me.

I don't expect that today will be the last time I experience the pit phenomenon. But when I experience it again, I pray that by God's grace I will recognize it as a challenge to grow more and more into the likeness of Jesus.

Meditation

Remain in me, as I in you.
As a branch cannot bear fruit all by itself,
unless it remains part of the vine,
neither can you unless you remain in me.
I am the vine,
you are the branches.
Whoever remains in me, with me in him,

bears fruit in plenty;
for cut off from me you can do nothing.

(John 15:4–5, NJB)

Reflection

Have I ever experienced the pit phenomenon in regard to my
ministry? What might have caused it?

Prayer

Lord, you have given me a wonderful gift: the chance to tell
others about your love. Sometimes I feel so excited about it that
I welcome the opportunities to share my time and my life with
others. More often than not, I receive much more than I think I
am giving.

But you also know that sometimes I am scared of failing or
that I am just plain selfish with my time. Sometimes I want to
punch out on a time card and say, "No one can expect anything
from me tonight. I'm off duty!"

Help me, Lord, to find the balance I need in my life. Help
me to recognize the times I am being selfish. Free me from my
preoccupation with being "good," and teach me to find my
security, my home, in you. Amen.

Oh No, It's Him!
When a Young Person Avoids You

Early in youth work I learned that if I want to reach out to young people who are outside of the church's programs or influence, I have to spend a great deal of time just hanging around where they are. For me, this means spending time at the high school. Being there after school hours or during a practice is a great way to see young people you know and to meet new kids. Sometimes, however, hanging around the high school can be awkward and uncomfortable for me or, as was the case today, for one of the young people.

This afternoon I went to watch the boys' cross-country meet. Watching the meet was only natural since three of the runners are in our youth group, and two of them are the top runners on the team. I really enjoy these guys, and I feel like I have a good relationship with each of them. They have always seemed to appreciate the fact that I come out to their meets, because not many people do.

Being a fan at a cross-country meet is a strange experience: you stand around waiting for the race to begin, and when it starts, the racers all run into the woods. Then you stand around for about seventeen minutes or so, trying to keep warm, until they come back. You've got to get all of your yelling in at the beginning and at the end. Sometimes I am the only fan at these meets and, I must admit, it can be kind of embarrassing to be screaming all by myself.

Anyway, today I couldn't help but notice that Mark seemed to avoid me. As I stood shooting the breeze with some of the other guys, he stood at a distance. When I finally caught his eye and said "Hi," he began to blush and became apologetic for not making it to the last two meetings at my house. He told me that he had dreaded seeing me at the meet and that he felt really guilty about not coming to the meetings.

I was completely surprised by Mark's reaction. Yes, I had noticed that he had not been at our meetings, and I did care about that. But it bothered me that my presence at his race translated into guilt feelings for him, as though I was there to indict him. I did not want that! I bent over backward trying to assure Mark that my presence at the race was not intended to make him feel uncomfortable. It was awful to find out my anticipated presence could be so foreboding for a young person—not exactly what I was hoping for.

Today's episode forces me to deal with my motives. Could I possibly be using my presence at the high school or at athletic events as a kind of bargaining chip with kids? I would like to think that my intentions are pure, that I go into the world of teenagers unconditionally, hoping to communicate Christ's love in all that I do and say. I don't want kids to see me and say: "Oh, no! There's Dan. . . . He must want us to come to one of his deals. He must be here trying to recruit kids for his group." It hurts me when I sense young people interpreting my presence that way. But I've got to wonder why they sometimes feel that way when I am around.

Outreach ministry has to be a ministry with no strings attached. Yes, I am going to the high school to see young people. Yes, I wouldn't mind if establishing relationships with them led them to desire to take part in the programs that I am running. After all, my hope is that the young people I know and work with will respond personally to the invitation to follow Jesus—and my programs are intended to offer that challenge. Like anyone else in youth work, I suppose I would be elated if I were faced with the problem of having to take on hundreds of kids who want to get involved—a problem I have never had.

Yet, what if they don't come? What if I develop good relationships, but some of them never set foot in one of my meetings or activities? Will I still value their friendships, still spend time with them outside of my events? And at an even deeper level, what if a kid does come, gets involved, and then decides that it is not for him or her? Will I still hang out with this kid? Still love this young person unconditionally? Isn't this the test of authentic love?

Meditation

To love at all is to be vulnerable. Love anything, and your heart will certainly be wrung and possibly be broken. If you want to make sure of keeping it intact, you must give your heart to no one, not even to an animal. Wrap it up carefully round with hobbies and little luxuries; avoid all entanglements; lock it up safe in the casket or coffin of your selfishness. But in that casket—safe, dark, motionless, airless—it will change. It will not be broken; it will become unbreakable, impenetrable, irredeemable. The alternative to tragedy, or at least to the risk of tragedy, is damnation. The only place outside Heaven where you can be perfectly safe from all the dangers and perturbations of love is Hell. (C. S. Lewis, *The Four Loves*, p. 169)

Reflection

How do young people react to my presence on their turf? Am I honest about my reasons for being there? With myself? With young people?

Prayer

Lord, I want kids to know that I am seeking them out in friendship because I care about them and not, primarily, my programs. I confess to you that occasionally I have spent time with young people only because I thought it was necessary to remind them of a meeting or event coming up. Help me to examine any hidden agendas I may carry with me when I am around young people and to keep my motives pure and up-front.

Jesus, you gave yourself freely in love. Help me to give myself away unconditionally to kids, to risk for love, so that just as you are the Good News in people's lives, I too might be good news in young people's lives. Amen.

◆ 3 ◆

No One Ever Told Me:
About Fifteen-Year-Old Girls

Every Halloween a friend of mine in ministry directs a big spookhouse fund-raising project called "Scream in the Dark." The project has become very popular in the last few years, with dozens of church youth groups from around the area participating. The whole effort takes quite a few people and several weeks' worth of volunteer hours.

One of the goals of the project, beyond fund-raising, is to spend some good times with young people while building and running the house. Scores of kids contribute to "Scream," and their biggest contribution comes during the actual running of the house, when they play various roles, such as Dracula, frog-creatures, escaped gorillas, ankle-grabbers, and so forth. It's a lot of fun.

This year I was asked to coordinate the assigning of roles each night before "Scream" opened. What happens is this: If a young person wants to play a part on a given night, he or she must show up an hour before the opening. Then we do everything we can to give him or her a role. It is usually a little crazy, with kids lobbying for favorite roles or asking to work with their friends in a certain room, but in the end it always seems to work out. Always, that is, until last night.

Last night Sarah was late. She arrived fifteen minutes before the spookhouse was to open, hoping to be given a role. When I told her that she was too late—all of the roles were filled—she became quite upset and began to plead with me. I explained that I could do nothing to change the situation: she was way too late. Everyone was already assigned and in place, and besides, I was busy trying to coordinate the whole thing and didn't have time to stand around trying to console her.

Sarah followed me around for an hour. I kept trying to act busy—which was easy—in order to avoid her. She kept badgering me: "Can't I please have a part? What am I supposed to do for two hours?" After telling her over and over that I did not have anything for her to do, I finally turned on her and said: "Sarah, stop whining at me! I am getting tired of hearing it! Now grow up and stop following me around!"

For the rest of the night Sarah sat in a corner and sulked, throwing me hurt looks that I pretended not to see. I was frustrated and annoyed with her. I wondered: *Am I really an ogre who lacks compassion?* I wish I hadn't yelled at Sarah, but I could not help myself. She was really acting like a spoiled brat.

Sarah is a sophomore whom I have known for a few months. When I got into youth work, no one ever told me about sophomores like Sarah. In fact, I would have to say that *some* freshmen and sophomore girls are quite difficult for me to deal with. I don't usually think of them when I am trying to feel good about myself as a youth worker. I would rather have serious root canal work done than have to sit in a room for an extended period of time with some of the freshmen and sophmore girls I know. I know that's not nice, not good, not compassionate. But it is the honest confession of a sometimes impatient, adult male who has never experienced what it means to be fifteen and female.

Does God ever feel like lashing out at someone? I felt like that last night. Today I am left wondering about my response to Sarah and how it all fits in with who I want to be in my relationship with her. How can I be good news in Sarah's life? How can I reflect God's love in my life to Sarah when last night all I wanted to do was yell at her, give her a swift kick in the rear end, and be rid of her?

I am aware, as I reflect on the events of last night, of God's incredible patience with me. How often have I sulked in a corner when I haven't gotten my way with God?

Does God ever feel like lashing out at someone? Thank you, God, for outlasting your feelings.

Meditation

Bless Yahweh, O my soul.
Bless God's holy name, all that is in me!
Bless Yahweh, O my soul,
and remember God's faithfulness:
in forgiving all your offenses,
in healing all your diseases,
in redeeming your life from destruction,
in crowning you with love and compassion.

· ·

Yahweh is merciful and forgiving,
slow to anger, rich in love;
Yahweh's wrath does not last forever;
it exists a short time only.
We are never threatened, never punished
as our guilt and our sins deserve.
. . . .
Yahweh knows what we are made of;
Yahweh remembers that we are dust.

(Ps. 103:1–14, Psalms Anew)

Reflection

Who are the young people in my life right now that I have
trouble being patient with? How can I best relate to them?

Prayer

Lord, if you dealt with me according to my behavior, I would be
in real trouble! I give praise to you, in true thanksgiving, for the
merciful and patient manner in which you love me and stay
faithful to me.

God, help me to treat others with the same measure of love.

Help me to grow in grace:
to forgive, as you forgive;
to be patient, as you are patient;
to laugh, as you laugh,
to love, as you love.
Amen.

❖ 4 ❖

Disappointing Others: Learning to Live with It

Experience has taught me that I will never be able to please all of the people all of the time. In fact, I have met people who never seem to be pleased with anything I do. The truth is that I want people to like me, so I always find it difficult when I know that a person is disappointed in me.

A few years ago, when I was on the part-time staff of Young Life, I became acquainted with a high school sophomore named Todd, who also happened to belong to my parish. Todd was not very interested in church or God or Young Life meetings. The intensity and energy that made him immediately likable was directed mainly toward girls and parties.

Todd's mother, Char, was a high-profile personality in our community and was very involved in the parish. The only way I can describe her is to say that upon encountering her, you felt as though you had been struck by a tornado. She was energy incarnate: hard to keep up with, concerned about many things, strongly opinionated, and oftentimes insensitive in her blunt-ness.

One of Char's chief concerns was Todd. She did not like many of his friends, felt he was doing poorly in school, and generally seemed unhappy about the choices he was making. Because of my volunteer work at the parish and my role with Young Life, Char, unfortunately for me, began to assume that I had messianic powers that could save Todd.

I don't think it is all that uncommon for Christian youth workers to find themselves faced with desperate parents groping for help with their kids. Parents sometimes try to transfer their responsibilities, which they may feel they have failed to carry out, onto the youth minister. It is as though they are saying, "You! You understand teenagers and are paid to influence them in healthy ways. Save my kid!"

Todd came to Young Life events because his mom made him come, and in the summer before his junior year, she made him go on a week-long trip to a Young Life camp. I think Todd had a great time at camp—girls came from five different states. He stayed somewhat aloof to the spiritual input and, in a very frank conversation at the end of the week, told me that he believed in God but was not ready to do anything with that because he did not want anything to interfere with his plans to "have a good time." At the end of the summer, Todd's parents rather abruptly told him that he was going away to a prep school—and Todd was gone.

In January of the next year, I received a phone call from Char, whom I had not seen for some time. She was extremely upset with me because of the way I had just "dropped" Todd. She let me know how disappointed she was in me—she must have said that ten times—for not writing to Todd during the fall term and for not trying to visit him while he was home during the Christmas break. She also used the occasion to let me know how disappointed she and her husband had been when I failed to report on how the week had gone for Todd at camp the previous summer. They had expected me to give them an inside perspective of how Todd had responded.

I was flabbergasted by the call, totally caught off-guard. My reaction was predictably defensive: I told her that I felt she might have exaggerated the extent of my relationship with Todd. Actually, I had not gotten all that close to Todd.

But no matter what I said, she simply repeated, "Well, I just have to tell you how disappointed I am in you." She did an extraordinary job of making me feel guilty.

Although I felt guilty, I did not trust my guilt. I knew how manipulative Char could be, and in her attack on me I could hear a refusal to embrace what she sensed were her own failures as a parent. It became clear by the end of the conversation that she was expecting me to apologize to her, but I could not do that. Each time she told me how disappointed she was, I simply responded that I was sorry she felt so disappointed.

The call left me feeling fragile, so I discussed the episode with my wife and with some colleagues on our leadership team. We talked about Char, about her expectations, and about my guilt feelings. I did a pretty good job of punishing myself for not having thought of writing to Todd at his school.

In the end, I was forced to accept the fact that I am not always going to be able to live up to the expectations that others have of me, and that there will always be people who will be disappointed with something I do or fail to do. Many times I won't be able to do anything about it. Not everybody is going to like me, understand the situations I work in, or appreciate my efforts.

The question for me then becomes, How can I live with this reality? With situations like the one with Char, my response will be, "You have my permission to be disappointed in me. I don't like your disappointment at all, but I guess we are both going to have to live with it."

I have felt a sense of liberation ever since I began to grant that kind of permission to others and to myself.

Meditation

> Let nothing trouble you,
> Let nothing scare you,
> All is fleeting,
> God alone is unchanging.
> Patience
> Everything obtains.
> Who possesses God
> Nothing wants.
> God alone suffices.
>
> (Saint Teresa of Ávila, *The Collected Works of St. Teresa of Ávila*, vol. 3, p. 386)

Reflection

Are there people in my life who always seem disappointed in me? How do I respond to these people?

Prayer

Lord, I wish that I could please everyone, but I can't. It bothers me when I know that someone is disappointed or angry with me. Help me to live with the fact that there will always be people in my life who are not completely happy with me.

God, I do want to please you. I know that at times even you are disappointed with me. But I do want to be honest in my relationship with you, to confront the times when I have failed, and to avail myself of your endless mercy. Lord, examine me and gently call me back to you. I make this prayer in the name of Jesus, the Way, the Truth, and the Life. Amen.

❖ 5 ❖
A Major "Dis":
Struggling with Rejection

One of the fun things about youth work is that if you know a few high school kids and hang around where they hang around, pretty soon you will get to know a lot of high school kids. Because peers are so important to young people during their adolescent years, when you get involved in one young person's life, you have a pretty good opportunity to meet her or his friends.

Andy and Chris have been good friends for a long time, and they are popular guys in their high school junior class. You might even say that they are two of the biggest hotshots on campus—and in their own minds! I met Chris while watching Andy practice track last spring. Both he and Andy are pole vaulters, and as Andy and I talked or joked around between vaults, Chris would often hang around and join in. I got to know and like Chris; he is outgoing and friendly.

Last night I ran into Chris at the local convenience store. As I was going in, he was coming out with some other guys that I didn't recognize. When I realized it was him, I gave him a smile and a warm greeting.

"Hey Chris! How you doin'?"

He did not show any sign of being excited to see me. He responded indifferently and with a tone of slight annoyance, "What?"

"I said, Hey! How's it going?"

Without breaking stride on his way out past me he muttered an almost inaudible "Hey," and was gone.

I really felt ignored. To use a term currently popular with the kids I know, this was a major "dis" on Chris's part. I had definitely been "dissed." I felt angry. I found myself thinking: *Well, I didn't come to the store to be totally blown off by Chris! Who the hell does he think he is anyway!*

The experience was also painful. Why did Chris ignore me and pretend he didn't know me? When I see him with Andy at practice or just hanging around the school, it seems like he goes out of his way to say hello. Now, here, when he's with different friends, he acts like he doesn't know me.

I felt confused and rejected. Even though I think I know better than to take something like a slight rejection from an adolescent personally, I did so. I even became immature in my interior response. *Screw it!* I thought. *If Chris wants to play games with me, I'm not going to put out a lot of effort in our relationship. He can't do that to me!*

Rejection can be very painful. It can immobilize any intention to reach out to others. Taking risks in a relationship is difficult when you feel paralyzed by the fear of rejection. I have struggled with this in my own life for many years. I think we all long to be loved, to be affirmed, and to be appreciated for who we are and for what we have to offer others. Rejection, real or imagined, is the antithesis of this yearning. When I feel accepted, it is much easier to let myself be known as I really am, to stand transparent before another.

When I feel rejected, I am apt to close myself up and hide behind protective walls. These walls have different guises. I can become a very busy person, with many appointments and meetings, who does not have the time to follow up on relationships that start to take place. Or I can preoccupy myself with self-centered projects that suddenly become more important than taking time to reach out to others. My prayer too becomes self-centered. I am not able to intercede for others, especially those who I feel have mistreated me.

Meditation

Meanwhile Peter was sitting outside in the courtyard, and a servant-girl came up to him saying, "You, too, were with Jesus the Galilean." But he denied it in front of them all. "I do not know what you are talking about," he said. When he went out to the gateway another servant-girl saw him and said to the people there, "This man was with Jesus the Nazarene." And again, with an oath, he denied it, "I do not know the man." A little later the bystanders came up and said to Peter, "You are certainly one of them too! Why, your accent gives you away." Then he started cursing and swearing, "I do not know the man." And at once the cock crowed, and Peter remembered what Jesus had said, "Before the cock crows you will have disowned me three times." And he went outside and wept bitterly. (Matt. 26:69–75, NJB)

Reflection

How does being rejected or disowned, whether it is real or imagined, affect me?

Prayer

Lord, you know how it feels to be disowned, even by your friends. But it is amazing how difficult it is for me to endure the slightest of rejections from a friend. Teach me to more readily embrace the little sufferings that come my way, thereby sharing in your passion in some small way.

Jesus, the reason I have come to know Chris, and others like him, is because of my love for you. I spend time with kids because you have invited me to love them in your name. Help me to remain faithful to that calling and to remember that you call me not to great success but to love and to care the best that I can. Amen.

❖ 6 ❖
Mom Knows Best?
When Parents Are Strange

I saw Tami at the track meet today. My wife and I came to know Tami through Young Life events, and last year I would have said that Tami was one of the high school kids we felt closest to. We spent a week together at a camp during the summer, saw her twice weekly—at a large-group meeting and in a smaller prayer group that met in our home—plus many more times just hanging around. I can think of more than one occasion last year when Tami stopped at our home just to visit. A few of those visits resulted in some pretty significant, spontaneous conversations about her life and faith journey.

Today, we had only a few minutes to chat before Tami had to leave. That's the way it has been most of this year. We don't see Tami very often anymore, only briefly now and then at the high school, and then she always seems to be in a hurry to get somewhere else. I am sad about this because I used to feel close to Tami.

What has happened is hard to say, but I do have some clues. About six months ago, on Easter Sunday, Tami's mom telephoned me for one of the most bizarre conversations I have ever had with a parent. She began by expressing concern about Tami not doing as well in school as she and her husband would like. (I should note that both of Tami's parents are successful doctors; I am also aware that Tami has never received a grade lower than an *A–*.) Tami's mother proceeded to list a number of the most prestigious colleges in the nation that she and Tami's father wanted Tami to apply to. Her concern, I finally learned, was that Tami was spending too much time in "these youth meetings" we were having, and that she feared this would jeopardize the college plans they had made for their daughter.

I had not gotten more than three words in during this conversation, and I was thinking: *Wow! What a neurotic, driven woman!*

I tried to explain to Tami's mom how we attempted to schedule our meetings in a way that would be sensitive to students' study needs, and I assured her that I would never want to see Tami's grades suffer as a result of her participation in our youth programs.

The conversation then took an about-face. This mother, whom I had never met, now began to complain to me about her daughter: how irresponsible she was around the house, how naive she was about colleges, how idealistic she was in her religious faith. I found myself gently defending Tami, whom I have always known to be responsible and friendly.

Then came the zinger: Tami's mom launched into a long, disjointed defense of her own religious faith. She told me of the many hours she had spent helping people, the years she had volunteered for this or that effort, and the sacrifices she had made for her family.

I was dumbfounded. I kept affirming this woman, assuring her that I did believe that she had done quite a bit, but all the while I was thinking: *Why is she telling me all of this? Where is this stuff coming from?*

In wondering about all this later, I began to suspect that Tami's mom was feeling threatened by her daughter's blossoming faith in Jesus and was, perhaps, feeling guilty over the way she was presently living out her own faith.

This was new to me. I had never experienced this in a parent before. If Tami's mom was feeling threatened and guilty and was subconsciously seeking to divert Tami from youth ministry events "for Tami's academic and future good," then she has been successful. Tami cannot go out on weeknights this year. Her mother is controlling Tami's life right now, and Tami, understandably, protects her mom by pretending to agree that the new arrangement is for the best.

I feel sorry for Tami, and for myself, because a friend has been taken out of my life.

Meditation

The difficult task of parenthood is to help children grow to the freedom that permits them to stand on their own feet, physically, mentally and spiritually and to allow them to move away in their own direction. The temptation is, and always remains, to cling to our children, to use them for our own unfulfilled needs and to hold on to them, suggesting in many direct and indirect ways that they owe us so much. (Henri J. M. Nouwen, *Reaching Out,* p. 78)

Reflection

Do I know any families or parents who seem to be diverting a son or daughter away from his or her responses to Jesus? What responsibilities do I have in such cases?

Prayer

God, I feel frustrated when I see a young person whose growth in faith seems to be stunted by a parent. It hurts to know that a young friend might be pulled away from you by the expectations of parents who think they are doing the best thing for their child.

Lord, sometimes it is hard to accept the parents or families that come along with young people. Yet I know that this is the only way they come! Continue to teach me how to nurture the faith of young people who find their commitment to Jesus running counter to their commitment to their families. Give me the sensitivity to know what to do and the courage to follow through. Amen.

❖ 7 ❖

Struggling in the Parish:
Youth Ministers Looking for Support

A number of youth ministers in our archdiocese meet once each
month to pray together, to support each other, and to share
resources. I find these times to be important for me personally,
and as a diocesan staff person, I am especially aware of how
valuable these few hours are to many of our parish youth
workers. I realize how isolated some youth ministers feel in
their parishes.

Of the many concerns that emerged at our last meeting,
two issues seemed to touch everyone in the group. First, recognition and acceptance as part of the parish staff is often withheld from laypersons in full-time youth ministry—withheld
particularly from women, and withheld particularly by priests.
Education and experience seem to make little difference in
whether a person is recognized and accepted. Those with
pastoral or youth ministry degrees, or with years of experience,
are, in most cases, no better off than some of the younger, less-
experienced youth ministers.

Second, parish leaders and adult parishioners often heap
enormous expectations on youth ministers. Our group generally felt that adult parishioners often expect the youth minister to
produce outcomes for their young people that far exceed the
outcomes that the efforts of the entire parish community
produce in the adults. The group interpreted the adult parishioners' expectations for their children as being a displacement
for their own unmet needs in the church.

In my diocesan position, I am becoming more and more
aware of the lack of recognition and support experienced by
many parish youth ministers. One of the most frustrating parts
of my job is watching gifted, effective youth ministry people
burn out because of lack of support from parish leadership. It is
not a revelation to say that there are pastors who do not give a
rip about youth ministry; that there are clergy who run their
parishes like small kingdoms, imagining themselves as rulers to
be served and feeling threatened by any initiative from anyone
other than themselves. This is not news. Yet dealing with it
regularly makes me angry and, at the same time, sad. Angry,
because true pastoral leadership is "to equip the saints for the

work of ministry, for building up the body of Christ" (Eph. 4:11–12, NRSV), not to stand in the way. And sad, because this pastoral posture often deprives young people of hearing and experiencing the Gospel in a dynamic and evangelizing way.

My sense is that this problem is not unique to Catholic parishes. During my years with Young Life, I often felt alone. I yearned to be more fully recognized and accepted, both within the organization itself and especially within the communities where I was ministering.

Too many of my friends are out there going it alone, and I honestly don't know how they are surviving. In fact, if the statistics are accurate, many are not surviving. These statistics show that people in youth ministry generally do not stay longer than two years. I don't think they leave simply because working with adolescents is hard. It is hard. But I think most leave out of discouragement.

Youth ministers are hired, are expected to know what to do and how to do it well, and then are often left on their own. Most, in the Catholic church anyway, have no supervisory relationship with a mentor who will help them plan and evaluate their ministry. Most have no one who will regularly listen to them, think problems through with them, and affirm them.

Someone recently said to me, "In youth ministry, the first six months you are new; after that, you are just stupid." It is too bad that so many people in youth ministry have been convinced of that.

Meditation

> It was a chilly, overcast day when the horseman spied the little sparrow lying on its back in the middle of the road. Reining in his mount he looked down and inquired of the fragile creature, "Why are you lying upside down like that?"
>
> "I heard the heavens are going to fall today," replied the bird.
>
> The horseman laughed. "And I suppose your spindly legs can hold up the heavens?"
>
> "One does what one can," said the little sparrow. (Source unknown, quoted in *Peacemaking: Day by Day* [Pax Christi USA], p. 61)

Reflection

From whom do I need acceptance and recognition to enable my ministry?

Prayer

God, youth ministry can sometimes be very lonely work. It is easy to get discouraged when I don't feel appreciated, and it frustrates me when so few—even in the church—seem to value ministry to young people.

Please lead me to people who will support me and believe in the ministry I have. Help me to find a community that will offer me encouragement and challenge me to grow. Bring to my mind those around me who may be experiencing loneliness and discouragement in their work, that I might offer encouragement to them. Amen.

Part 2

◆

DISCERNMENT

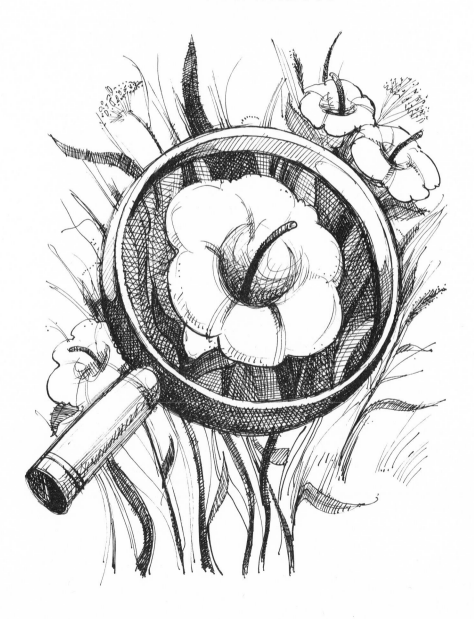

◆ **8** ◆

How Am I Doing?
Measuring Success in Ministry

One of the privileges of being in diocesan work is getting to meet so many wonderful people involved in parish youth ministry. I have become aware of things that bring joy to their work, as well as things that prove to be difficult. A phone conversation with Anna this morning touched on one of those difficult things.

Anna is a full-time youth minister in an urban parish. She has been in the parish for only one year and will be leaving in a few months to continue her education at a nearby graduate school. I've known for some time that the situation in her parish is not a great one. Anna was hired as the first, full-time professional youth minister but was never given full charge of the youth program. A woman who preceded her continues to hold a tight grip on the senior high youth group, and the priests in the parish have done little to change that.

I think Anna has done remarkably well in her one year at the parish, considering the situation she stepped into. While she has not been able to successfully assert herself as the coordinator of the senior high group, Anna has done an admirable job with the junior high youth. Through her strong relational skills, her love for Christ, and her commitment to these young people, she has created a place and a reason for about thirty junior high kids to come together.

This morning Anna shared with me some of her feelings about leaving the parish. Although she is excited about her school plans for the fall, the undercurrent that ran throughout our talk was Anna's sense of failure, the feeling that she had not accomplished anything in her year at the parish. Looking back on the year, she saw mostly what she had been unable to do, rather than what she had accomplished. She wondered if her year had been wasted. She felt she was letting down the parish by leaving so soon, and more deeply, she questioned whether she was letting down God by spending a whole year at that parish with seemingly so little to show for it.

It was a tough day for Anna. I have had my share of tough days, and my guess is that everyone in ministry has them. I am not sure how helpful I was to Anna on the phone this morning, but two things occurred to me while I was talking with her, and they have stayed with me all day.

First, in youth (or any) ministry, it is so important to keep results in their proper perspective. One year is a short time to be in a parish, and there is only so much you can expect to accomplish in one year, especially a first year.

Second, from what I could see, Anna had accomplished a lot. Foremost in my mind was the great love and commitment she displayed. She struck me as someone who wants to learn, someone who wants to give the best to the kids she is working with. She is always honest about her limitations and earnest in pursuing people that she thinks can help her to grow. She loves Jesus, she loves kids, and they love her.

Had she done everything that needed to be done in the parish? No. Had she successfully worked with the woman controlling the senior high group? No. Could she be certain that the junior high group she had begun would hold together after she was gone? No. But she had done her best in the short time she was there and had some important accomplishments. She had done it with love. And she had learned a lot. Result: a successful year.

A reality for youth ministers (and again, probably for all ministers) is that they often wonder about their effectiveness. Rarely are there big, measurable results. In ministry, one can't come home in the evening like a commissioned salesperson and say, "Well, today I did almost twice as good as I did all last week!" There aren't many reliable charts or graphs you can keep in ministry. What does one count: The number of people who come? The number of conversions? The money? I'll take all three! Yet, can one be successful in all of these but still be failing as a minister of the Gospel?

I don't pretend to know what makes a person's ministry successful. But I think success might have something to do with gradually letting go of all those external indicators while growing more and more dependent on God's grace, power, and mercy in all that we do.

Meditation

Do not depend on the hope of results. When you are doing the sort of work you have taken on, essentially an apostolic work, you may have to face the fact that your work will be apparently worthless and even achieve no result at all. . . . As you get used to this idea, you start more and more to concentrate not on the results but on the value, the rightness, the truth of the work itself. And there too a great deal has to be gone through, as gradually you struggle less and less for an idea and more and more for specific people. The range tends to narrow down, but it gets much more real. In the end, it is the reality of personal relationships that saves everything.

. . . the big results are not in your hands or mine, but they suddenly happen, and we can share in them; but there is no point in building our lives on this personal satisfaction, which may be denied us and which after all is not that important. (Letter from Thomas Merton, in James H. Forest, *Thomas Merton's Struggle with Peacemaking* [Pax Christi USA], pp. 41–42)

Reflection

How do I measure success in my ministry?

Prayer

Lord, it is often hard to know whether my work with young people is successful. How can I really know? Sometimes I wish that my ministry could be measured like assembly-line work in a factory or that I had some kind of quota system I could use to evaluate myself.

I depend on you, God. I know I cannot always trust my feelings when it comes to evaluating my ministry. I commit all that I am and all that I do to you, asking you to redeem it and bless it so that it might bring you glory. I pray this in the name of your Son, Jesus Christ. Amen.

You @#$%&! Kids:
Getting Angry at Young People

I have just returned from a weekend youth retreat. Something happened to me during the weekend that has never happened before, at least not to the degree that I experienced it this past Saturday night. I absolutely blew up at the guys in my dorm.

Ten of us shared our dorm room for the weekend: eight guys, another adult leader, and me. I know these kids well, and I like them . . . for the most part. Of the eight guys, six are knitted closely together in a clique built almost entirely upon the practice of mutual put-downs and ridicule. These guys constantly hassle each other, daily forming new alliances within the group, waging verbal war against each other. It seems as though each one's self-esteem is dependent upon cutting others down in order to make himself feel good. Sometimes it's maddening to be around this constant battling.

On Friday night this clique was in the middle of an intense pillow fight, with a fire extinguisher involved in the melee at one point.

By Saturday morning the adult leaders from the different parishes had put their heads together and promised to make sure that this would not happen a second time. At lunch that day I talked with our guys about keeping things cool. Because our guys felt that the group in the dorm room next door had gotten the best of Friday night's go-around, they had devised a get-even plan. I made it clear that I expected them to cool it and suggested that we find a good-natured, less destructive way to get even.

That evening during a social hour I became aware that the six guys were still plotting something, so I pulled them aside and reminded them of our conversation at lunch. While affirming their spirit of adventure, I again asked them to cool it and communicated (I thought) my trust in them as they promised to abandon their scheme.

Within an hour of that last conversation, one kid was in bed with a bloody, broken nose—the result of a well-directed punch—and one mattress was smoldering outside. The contents of an empty fire extinguisher partly covered the body of the puncher, and a dorm room was turned completely upside down.

I was more than a little angry. As I stood looking out at the burning mattress, at the room where every piece of personal clothing had been taken out of every suitcase and thrown about, and at the mattresses pulled from the bed frames, rage swelled up in my throat. While the kid with the hemorrhaging nose lay gurgling on his bed, Jay, the puncher, stood there defending himself, explaining how all this had happened. Jay is at least twice as big as I am, and I have never been a fighter, but I envisioned myself sitting on top of him, choking him.

I took Jay and the other responsible guy to the destroyed room and formally introduced them to each individual whose belongings had been violated. After apologies were made, I suggested that those individuals recline on a mattress while I directed my two guys in the entire cleanup: every piece of clothing was folded and returned to the proper suitcase; every toothbrush, comb, and stick deodorant was put back where it belonged.

Then we went back to our dorm room to deal with the remaining culprits. When I got there, they were sort of cowering, looking at anything but me. I tried to remain in control; I talked about trust being betrayed, and I let my anger and disappointment show. When they began to justify what they had done and blame each other for what had happened, my self-control snapped. Considering the circumstances, how could they dare to talk back to me?

I became a raging monster, pacing in front of them, using just about every expletive I knew. I called them immature, irresponsible, and said that it was really a pain in the ass to be around them. I screamed about the way they treated each other, that I had never been involved with a group of guys so depressing. It was an impressive outburst. I could tell from the gaping mouths, wide eyes, and stiffened backs that I had their attention.

When I was through, I felt numb. I believed every word I had said was on target, but there was also a sinking feeling: *Oh my God, what have I done?* I had never become that angry with kids before. I thought I might as well write off any spiritual benefits from the weekend, as well as my relationship with these guys. I had let my anger get the best of me, no question. Now I wondered if there was anything to salvage, whether any of the guys would ever talk to me again.

Later that night in the bathroom, as the others shuffled around me, gargling and spitting, one of our guys came up to me and thanked me. I was caught by surprise; I began to apologize out of embarrassment for the extent of my outburst, but he quickly assured me that what I had said, and the way I had said it, needed to be heard. That made me feel better, but I am still startled by the intensity of my angry outburst and especially by some of the saucy words I chose to express myself.

With the weekend behind, all is pretty much forgotten, and our relationships have remained intact. But I see how powerful a force anger can be, for good or for bad. I am sure it is usually disastrous when it is out of control like mine was. I thank God for the good that came out of it this time.

Meditation

> Be angry but do not sin; do not let the sun go down on your anger, and do not make room for the devil. (Eph. 4:26–27, NRSV)

Reflection

When was the last time I felt really angry with a young person? How did it turn out? Do I manage my anger well? How do I follow up after being angry?

Prayer

Jesus, I remember how, in your anger, you trashed the tables of the money changers in the Temple. It is easy for me to believe that my own anger is sometimes justified, even righteous. But how can I really know?

Anger can scare me, Lord. I don't like the feeling of losing control. I worry that my anger will alienate me from the very people I am called to serve.

Help me, Jesus,
to discern correctly while I am angry;
to find healthy ways to express my anger;
to know when to let go of my anger and seek healing.
Amen.

❖ 10 ❖
Dark Night:
The Desert Experience

Yesterday I had lunch with Marti, a junior at a nearby college who has been involved as a volunteer on our team since her freshman year. She is energetic, bright, refreshing to be around, and kids really respond well to her. I'm glad she is on our leadership team.

At lunch, Marti talked about how dry her prayer life seemed to be. She expressed feelings of distance from God. Her times of prayer seemed fruitless; she was having trouble getting excited about spiritual reading, liturgy, or just about anything.

I asked Marti: "What do you expect to feel like? What do you think you can do about that dry feeling that has been plaguing you?" In the end we had to believe together that whether she could feel it or not, God was doing something beautiful in Marti's life right now. I was able to point out areas where I had seen significant growth over the two years I had known her, growth that Marti was not aware of until I brought it to her attention.

After listening to Marti, I realized how often, when asked about our prayer life, we complain that we are feeling dry or dead. Reflecting on my own experience, I find that during these "desert experiences," few of the disciplines of my spiritual life are appealing to my senses. During these times, it takes great resolve and effort to regularly make it to liturgy on Sunday. Feelings-wise, I would much rather take a leisurely shower, eat sweet rolls, and read the paper. I certainly do not want to fast, give money to poor people, serve Jesus in those who are suffering, confess my sins, reveal myself to a spiritual director, and live a simple life. Yet I know I have to continue to attempt these things if I want to keep in touch with Jesus. During these dry times, I—a lazy, selfish, gluttonous, justifying liar—have to force myself, usually with some pain, to carry out these disciplines.

The so-called desert experience or "dark night of the soul," as Saint John of the Cross experienced it, is not a rarity in our life with God. In my small experience, it is more often the norm. But the desert is not a place to flee. It is a place to recognize that if you are there, God is there too, pruning the dry and the dead to make room for the fresh and the living.

Meditation

This night and purgation of the desire, a happy one for the soul, works in it so many blessings and benefits (although to the soul, as we have said, it rather seems that blessings are being taken away from it) . . . even so is there joy in Heaven because God is now taking this soul from its swaddling clothes, setting it down from His arms, making it to walk upon its feet, and likewise taking from it the milk of the breast and the soft and sweet food proper to children, and making it to eat bread with crust, and to begin to enjoy the food of robust persons. (Saint John of the Cross, *Dark Night of the Soul*, p. 76)

Reflection

What happens when I stop feeling close to God? What disciplines can help me to stay rooted in Christ?

Prayer

Lord, I am grateful for the many times I have felt your intimate friendship and sensed your healing touch in my life. But you know, God, that many days I do not feel you close by. Help me, Lord, during these desert experiences, to remain faithful to my commitment to you. Keep me rooted, not in my feelings, but in your promise to never leave or forsake me. I make this prayer in the name of Jesus. Amen.

◆ 11 ◆

Mr. Nice Guy or Sergeant Discipline: Which One When?

Last night I spoke to a group of about seventy-five seventh and eighth graders in a parish I had never visited before. I was the speaker in the third week of a Lenten series the parish is running for young people. The comments I heard from some of the religious education teachers before I spoke led me to believe that things had not been going very well. "This is a hard group," they informed me. "If they sense you are vulnerable, they will really eat you up!" I listened politely, and as I looked over the crowd sitting obediently in rows of folding chairs, I saw that I-am-here-because-my-parents-made-me-come-and-I-would-much-rather-not-be-trapped-here-in-the-basement-of-the-church-listening-to-any-stupid-guest-speaker-talk-about-anything look on their faces.

I was not intimidated. I speak to groups quite frequently, and last night I guess I was feeling a little cocky. Things may not have gone well the last two weeks, but then, *I* didn't speak the last two weeks. I was pretty confident that I could win over even these "hard" kids.

I started with one of my best stories: riding up the chair lift with a woman who had a huge amount of snot hanging from her nose. Perfect stuff for a junior high crowd. They were riveted to their seats while I effectively grossed them out with the details of this encounter; I was really rolling. Occasionally an individual in the crowd would interrupt me, as junior high students are apt to do, to ask some irrelevant question:

"Did you throw up?"

"Huh, what's that? Ah, no, I didn't throw up. So anyway, we're riding up and I'm hoping that this snot won't fall on my coat. And . . ."

"Do you know if Mrs. Perry is taking us for pizza after this?"

"Ah, no, I don't. Try to hang with me here, gang. So anyway, it's getting colder and colder, see . . ."

Anyone who works with junior high kids knows that these kinds of disruptions are common; you have to roll with them. But when I picked up my Bible to make the transition from my personal story to the Gospel story I was going to share, a massive groan came from the group: "Ohhhhh!" You would have thought I had just informed them that the brownies they had eaten before the meeting were laced with poison. It was such a dramatic response, almost funny. The questions began again but with new fervor: "Is this a long story?" "Is this going to be boring?" "Can I go to the bathroom?" I just stood there, grinning incredulously. I had never heard protests come so aggressively.

Then I asked them pointedly what seemed like a good question at the time but proved to be a disaster: "Hey, would you rather be someplace else?" Immediately the eyes of the girls I was particularly addressing my question to widened, and they emphatically said, "*Yes! We want to go out for pizza!*"

Decision time. I had a split second to decide what I was going to do. The teachers, somewhat typically in my experience, had left the room at the beginning of my talk, and only God knew where they were. If it had been my group, I probably would have just quit and gone out for pizza. But here, I was the guest speaker. They invited me and were actually planning to pay me for my talk. I had to go on. So I put down my Bible and called for a time-out.

For the next two minutes I said basically the following: "Look, I drove a half-hour in the snow to come here because I was invited to talk to you. I like doing this. I could be at home with my family right now, but I chose to be here. If you don't want to listen to what I have to say, that's okay. You can tune out. But I want you to know that I think it is really rude for you to groan out loud at me while I am trying to share something I think is important. I can't make you listen to me, but I can ask that you act decently toward another human being and respect my feelings."

It worked. I finished with an abbreviated version of the second part of my talk, said my good-byes, and went home.

As I reflect on this experience, I realize that there is a fine line between knowing when to roll with young people and when to call a time-out, knowing when kids are just being kids and knowing when to put your foot down. To err on the one side is to be the eternal pushover. Some kids will attempt just about anything if they know they will never be called to responsible behavior. To err on the other side is to be the hardline disciplinarian, constantly scolding kids and keeping them in line.

Being the first kind of leader may result in having lots of friends among the youth, but a pushover is taken advantage of and ineffective in calling young people to any kind of maturity.

Being of the second breed may result in tightly controlled programs, but a hard-line disciplinarian has fewer friendships with young people. In either case, the Gospel message I want to convey doesn't go very far.

Young people need me to model the joy of laughter, to have fun with them, and even to be crazy with them. In fact, I think I have a responsibility to lead them in appropriate craziness! But they also need to see me model responsibility and compassion for others. The two are not so opposed as they might seem. I have the opportunity to lead them in both.

Meditation

Give a shepherd's care to the flock of God that is entrusted to you: watch over it, not simply as a duty but gladly, as God wants; not for sordid money, but because you are eager to do it. Do not lord it over the group which is in your charge, but be an example for the flock. When the chief shepherd appears, you will be given the unfading crown of glory. (1 Pet., 5:2–4, NJB)

Reflection

What is my posture with young people? Do I tend to be a pushover, or do I tend toward playing the authority figure? Can I create a healthy blend?

Prayer

Lord, you have called me as an adult to be a friend to young people. Part of that means just being with kids in the hilarity of youth, and part of it means calling them to a maturity that enables them to consider that they are not the only persons in the universe. Help me to discern the times when I should allow young people the latitude they need as youth and when I need to challenge them to grow up. Amen.

❖ 12 ❖
Telling Kids the Truth:
The Cost of Following Jesus

In the past few years I have had an increasing sense of the radical nature of the life that Jesus invites us to. As I see the value system spewed out by our materialistic, North American culture pull more and more on my own lifestyle, the way of Jesus described in the Gospels strikes me with its stark contrast. I recognize some of the little compromises with what I know to be the way of Christian discipleship that I make in my own life, and I also recognize some of these same compromises in my ministry.

I recently took part in a nearby diocesan youth convention. In the midst of dramas, workshops, general sessions, and meals, I found myself thinking: *We are not challenging these kids in any significant way. We carry on as if being a follower of Jesus is easy!* The convention was like a lot of conventions I have been to—affirming, action-packed, fun. It was actually a terrific convention. I enjoyed being part of it. Yet it occurred to me, probably because of my own sense of struggling to follow Jesus in an authentic way, that something of the Gospel message was missing.

I don't think that this is a unique situation limited to large Catholic youth conventions. I see it in parish groups, on diocesan youth councils, and among Protestant youth groups I have contact with. And I don't think the issue is only for young people. Even more so, it is an issue for the adult church in the United States.

Where are the prophetic voices of our age, calling us to live dramatically different lives that run counter to the status quo of our society? Do the people in my parish live differently from the rest of the people in my community? How many who leave parishes or congregations do so because they are disillusioned by the apparent failure of the members to follow Jesus? It is hard for me to even pose these questions, as the mediocrity of my own discipleship to Christ flies in my face.

Our culture invites us to value power, to value money, to value pleasure, to value individualism. In contrast, it seems to me that Jesus invites us to value service, to value simplicity, to value joy, to value community. As much as anyone, I am lured

by the attraction of our culture's values even as I struggle daily
to follow Jesus. And it is a daily struggle.

Like many adults, many young people compartmentalize
their life so that their religious life never comes into contact
with the other areas of their existence. Yet the very concept of
lordship, which Jesus claims over us, implies that every area of
my life will be infiltrated and subject to evaluation by Jesus. My
vocation, my economics, my sexuality, my politics, my social
behavior, my time—all will be affected forever by my decision
to follow the Jesus of the Gospels.

I realize that carrying the concept of the lordship of Jesus
into my ministry means that kids will sometimes think that I
am trying to spoil their Saturday nights. But they need to know
that a decision to follow Jesus includes much more than that—
so much more.

I believe that the countercultural Christ is an attractive
figure for many young people. In the years that I have done
Scripture study with kids, the most exciting times have been
encounters with the many hard sayings of Jesus. Kids stop
slouching and start listening when they hear Jesus turn everything upside down in the Sermon on the Mount.

I like to talk to young people about how much God loves
us. I will never stop talking about that. Yet if I am going to
evangelize young people responsibly, I have to be honest by
telling them what getting involved with Jesus entails. It's much
more than youth convention dances and making banners.
Ultimately, I have to trust that the Holy Spirit will lead them to
recognize that following Jesus is a life of adventure and community, whereas a life committed to the values of our culture is, in
the end, a life of boredom and loneliness.

Meditation

A Jewish convert, who had been making a retreat with us at
Maryfarm, said some weeks after, "It is hard to live in the
upside-down world of the Gospels." Truly it is a world of
paradoxes, giving up one's life in order to save it, dying to
live. It is voluntary poverty, stripping oneself even of what
the world calls dignity, honor, human respect. (Dorothy
Day, *Meditations*, p. 91)

Reflection

How might Jesus be calling me deeper, today, in my conversion to him?

Prayer

Lord Jesus Christ, Son of God, help me to be faithful to your way, your truth, your life. Help me to invite young people to follow you by my actions and by my words. When I fail, make sure that I become aware of it. Lord Jesus Christ, Son of God, have mercy on me, a sinner. Amen.

❖ 13 ❖

Busy, Busy:
Real Youth Ministers Have Time to Pray

This weekend I directed a retreat for eleven professional youth ministers from different parts of New England. This was a new experience for me. I had done all kinds of weekends with young people and had directed spiritual experiences for other adults, but I had never before been a director for my peers on a quiet retreat.

The twelve of us met together at a youth center, and from there we drove to the retreat house about twenty minutes away. In our conversation on the way to the house, it became clear that nearly every one of the youth ministers was feeling some anxiety about making a retreat at this particular time. They felt excitement and relief about the retreat, which they had been planning for months, but the obligations and tasks waiting back home were nagging at them too. Some talked about meetings they had had to cancel, others about the "crunch week" they anticipated when they returned. A few even mentioned that co-workers had given them some good-natured grief for taking this time to go on retreat. It became clear to me that while they really wanted this retreat, some were having to work hard to justify it to themselves or to others.

That first evening of the retreat, we talked about the fact that there is never a right time to make a retreat, and that this is perhaps the whole point. We spent time considering Martha and Mary as they experienced the visit of Jesus in their home. It was easy to see how well we played the part of Martha, and how difficult we found it to follow the example of Mary, who had chosen the "better part."

In youth work, I sometimes feel a great temptation, demonic in origin I am sure, to stay busy in order to feel productive. Like Martha, I become "distracted with all the serving" and fail to spend time simply sitting at the feet of Jesus, attentive, adoring. I become so overwhelmed by the tasks in my ministry that oftentimes at night when I lay down in bed I say "Hello, Lord" for the first time that day.

Imitating Mary is hard. Sitting quietly before Jesus is sometimes scary. Sitting before Jesus in solitude challenges me to look honestly at myself through his eyes, and I am asked to

trust him in all of my nakedness. It is surrender. It is abandon-
ment. If I stay busy, I keep control. If I sit with Jesus, I give all
things up.

Meditation

In the course of their journey he came to a village, and a
woman named Martha welcomed him into her house. She
had a sister called Mary, who sat down at the Lord's feet
and listened to him speaking. Now Martha, who was
distracted with all the serving, came to him and said, "Lord,
do you not care that my sister is leaving me to do the
serving all by myself? Please tell her to help me." But the
Lord answered, "Martha, Martha," he said, "you worry and
fret about so many things, and yet few are needed, indeed
only one. It is Mary who has chosen the better part, and it
is not to be taken from her." (Luke 10:38 – 42, NJB)

Reflection

Can I afford to spend a whole day or weekend in quiet prayer?
When will I do it?

Prayer

Lord, as a youth minister I will always be busy with things to
do. Your call to come away for a little while, to spend an hour, a
day, a weekend, or even longer in prayer, reflection, and spiritual dialog, can get muffled by my anxiety to feel productive. I
need to be reminded of the "better part" of my ministry, and I
pray that the better part will increasingly precede all of the
other "big" things that I do in your name. Amen.

❖ 14 ❖
Busy, Busy:
Real Youth Ministers Make Time to Play

Yesterday was my son's third birthday. Originally we were going to spend the day at an amusement park nearby, but we found out that it was closed on weekdays. Because I had already set the day aside to be with my family, I spent it just hanging around at home. It was a beautiful spring day, and I enjoyed the time relaxing and playing with my family. But at the same time, during a few moments in my leisurely day, I felt some pangs of guilt.

A few years ago I read a book entitled *When I Relax I Feel Guilty.* I could have written that book. For reasons I can't fully explain, I sometimes suffer terribly from guilt when I am engaged in any kind of leisure activity. It is maddening to feel this guilt when I am sitting in a restaurant talking with a friend, when I am playing golf for an afternoon, or when I am shopping at a mall for socks and a pair of jeans. And it is just plain sad that I could feel twinges of guilt for being home on my son's birthday.

What makes me nervous about being discovered on the golf course, playing at the beach, or reading at home at a time when most other people are busy? Why am I embarrassed to be at home on a weekday at ten in the morning when a friend of my wife's calls on the phone: "Oh, why Dan, what are you doing at home?" Translation in my head: *Why aren't you doing something important? Why aren't you at the office like my husband and the rest of the fathers in our neighborhood who don't get home until six-thirty?*

On the one hand, I celebrate the fact that I don't have an office job that requires me to be away from my family from eight till six every weekday. I love the fact that my ministry responsibilities allow me to have a great deal of control over my schedule. On the other hand, if you ask me how my weekend was and if it involved many hours of ministry, chances are I'll let you know all about it, just so you know how busy I was. This helps me justify being at home on Tuesday mornings at ten.

In fact, I have more than my share of weekends and evenings away from home. Like so many others in our anxious society, I am too busy, too busy for my own good and the good of my family and friends.

I think God probably gets tired of busy people wrapped up in so much work, a lot of which is trivial, never taking time to dance and be foolish.

Today I am recommitting myself to not letting others, who are too uptight to play, make me feel guilty. I am going to "make merry" like David before the Lord (2 Sam. 6:14–21, NAB). I am going to play because I need to play and because playing is good. I am going to play and love and laugh while I can. Life is too short to not do so.

Meditation

If I had my life to live over again, I'd try to make more mistakes next time.

I would relax, I would limber up, I would be sillier than I have been this trip.

I know of very few things I would take seriously.

I would take more trips. I would be crazier.

I would climb more mountains, swim more rivers, and watch more sunsets.

I would do more walking and looking.

I would eat more ice cream and less beans.

I would have more actual troubles, and fewer imaginary ones.

You see, I'm one of those people who lives life prophylactically and sensibly hour after hour, day after day. Oh, I've had my moments, and if I had to do it over again I'd have more of them.

In fact, I'd try to have nothing, just moments, one after another, instead of living so many years ahead each day. I've been one of those people who never go anywhere without a thermometer, a hot-water bottle, a gargle, a raincoat, aspirin, and a parachute.

If I had to do it over again I would go places, do things, and travel lighter than I have.

If I had my life to live over I would start barefooted earlier in the spring and stay that way later in the fall.

I would play hookey more.

I wouldn't make such good grades, except by accident.

I would ride on more merry-go-rounds.

I would pick more daisies.

(Letter from an anonymous friar, written late in his life, quoted in Tim Hansel, *When I Relax I Feel Guilty*, pp. 44–45)

Reflection

Do I take time to have fun and relax? Do I allow, even encourage, peers to be spontaneous and playful?

Prayer

God of life, you have created me out of love and gifted me with life. All of creation rightly gives you praise and reveals your goodness and glory.

Open my eyes and free my heart so that I might truly see and enjoy you in every moment. May my life increasingly bring glory to you by my enjoyment of laughter, children, tall trees, music, and good beer and lasagna with friends. Amen.

Part 3

◆

PRIVILEGE

❖ 15 ❖
Breakfast with Sully:
Discovering
Where Real Ministry Happens

This morning I had breakfast with Sully, a senior in our group who is about to graduate and head off to college in the fall. I have known Sully for about two years. It is fun to spend time with him because he is a unique person in many ways. His clothing is offbeat, his hair is long, and the way he carries himself—especially when he dances—seems to communicate the message, "I am happy to be me and I am definitely not trying to be like anyone else." This is not a common attitude among most of the high school kids I know.

At breakfast this morning we talked about his plans for college, how he felt about leaving high school, how things were going at home, and eventually about his faith. Sully is a near genius when it comes to math and logic and all that stuff. I have had talks with him in which he has excitedly tried to explain some new thinking or theory in math, and I have just had to sit there with a silly grin on my face saying things like "hmmm . . ." and "ahh . . ." and "what?"

Our discussions about God and Jesus have always been fairly apologetic in nature: Was Jesus divine? Are miracles possible? Is Jesus the only way to God? I have always been impressed with Sully's honest search for truth and very real desire to place his faith in Jesus. In fact, he told me at breakfast that he wanted to talk because "I want to go to college as a believer, but I've got to deal with my doubts!"

I like to think that I can play the apologetic game pretty well. I studied *Five Ways* (by Thomas Aquinas) in college, I've read my share of Chesterton and C. S. Lewis, and I've had my share of "beer and bull" sessions during seminary. So I was comfortable mixing it up with Sully this morning. But just as we were getting warmed up on the question of whether Jesus was a liar, a lunatic, or the Truth, Sully switched gears on me.

"You know, I really hope that I can be a father some day." *Huh?*

"I think the times I have felt closest to God and most like a Christian have been the times when I have been able to just hang out at your house and see you and Sue with Joey and Julian."

Wait a minute! I thought. *What about all of our little discussions on the Trinity and the existence of God? And what about that excellent talk I gave last week at our meeting? What about the little thing I did on the parable of the sower that one time? You probably want to include those things too, don't you?*

I am learning more and more that kids aren't really impressed so much by the talks I give or the Scripture studies I do with them. I am sure those are important, but not nearly as important as I imagine them to be. What Sully is teaching me is that simply sharing my life is what really counts.

But close to God, in my home? All I could think of was screaming children, soiled diapers, tired parents, and cold pizza. But crying babies, dirty diapers, and cold pizza may do more to lead a friend toward Christ than all the talks given in a year. I am slowly realizing that most young people are not really looking for friendship with well-polished, perfect, Christian adults but with adults who are honestly trying to live the Gospel message and who are willing to share that attempt.

Maybe the best I have to offer in ministry is my small home, two wild little boys, and a marriage relationship that is sometimes glamorous but, for the most part, takes a lot of hard work and is still finding its way.

Meditation

Ministry means the ongoing attempt to put one's own search for God, with all the moments of pain and joy, despair and hope, at the disposal of those who want to join this search but do not know how. (Nouwen, *Creative Ministry,* p. 111)

Reflection

To what extent, and in what way, can I let young people in on my struggle to follow Jesus?

Prayer

Thank you, God, for the reminder that my life means more to the young people I know than my many words. Help me to be more generous in letting others in on my life, even with all of its messiness and rough edges. Let me remember that kids are not looking so much for a perfect Christian, a perfect marriage relationship, or a perfect home, but for people who are willing to share their lives as they struggle—with good humor—to live out their commitment to Christ. Amen.

❖ 16 ❖
And What Do You Do?
Being Identified as "Religious"

Today at a wedding reception I was asked a question that I suppose we are all asked at events like wedding receptions: "And what is it that you do?" When the woman asked, I told her I was involved in ministry to young people. She paused for about five seconds, kept her smile, and then responded, "Oh, well isn't that nice." She looked down at her drink and with another uneasy gulp asked further, "So, are these troubled kids that you work with, then?" By the time I explained my ministry and we finished with our conversation, I was not sure who wanted more to get away for another drink, the woman or me!

I am not sure why many people feel uneasy when I tell them that I am involved in ministry. For some, it seems that the mere mention of spiritual matters is taboo in a social setting. I sometimes feel awkward and uncomfortable in turn, especially in trying to explain what I do. I imagine it would be easier just to say that I work for an insurance company or an investment firm. Sometimes I feel like giving that answer so people wouldn't have to feel obliged to tell me how nice it all is.

It can be easy for those of us who are in ministry to buy into the value system of our secularized society that places such little value on something like youth ministry. When people look at us strangely and show signs of being uncomfortable in our presence, we may sometimes doubt that what we do is important, since we receive so little appreciation from the larger community around us.

I guess it is a fact that religious-sounding work and religious-sounding people do not fit in easily with mainstream careers and social life. But who ever said that being identified with Jesus was supposed to be commonly accepted? It never has. And yet, perhaps, this is what can make youth ministry so exciting!

Although at times I wish I could just tell people at wedding receptions that I drive a milk route, perhaps I should really fear the day when the words "I am a youth minister" are simply taken for granted.

Meditation

See what love the Father has given us, that we should be
called children of God; and that is what we are. The reason
the world does not know us is that it did not know him.
Beloved, we are God's children now; what we will be has
not yet been revealed. What we do know is this: when he is
revealed, we will be like him, for we will see him as he is.
And all who have this hope in him purify themselves, just
as he is pure. (1 John 3:1–3, NRSV)

Reflection

Have I ever felt clumsy identifying myself as a person involved
in ministry? When is it hardest for me to talk about my
ministry?

Prayer

Lord, sometimes it isn't fun or easy to be so closely identified
with you. There are so many awful stereotypes for "religious"
persons, and I feel that people sometimes just write me off
when they hear the word *ministry*. I like to be liked, and yet so
often I feel that people want to avoid me when they hear that I
am "religious."

Forgive me for the times I seek to be comfortable and
approved of at the cost of losing my identity in you. Keep me
rooted in the Gospel, Lord, and protect me from discouragement. Amen.

❖ 17 ❖

Proms and Zits:
Loving Young People Where They Live

My wife and I have developed a good friendship with Nancy, a high school junior in our parish. Nancy is popular with many of her classmates, and this spring she was one of the chairpersons of her class prom. For months, Nancy seemed to do nothing but eat, drink, sleep, and dream this prom into existence. The closer the date for the dance came, the more she fretted and worried. Not least among her anxieties was the fact that she did not have a date for the dance. To hear her talk, you would have guessed that if she was not asked to the prom soon—by the right guy, of course—she would be forced to move to another state under an assumed name.

I admit that I tired pretty quickly of hearing about Nancy's prom pressure. My wife was much more understanding. She listened willingly as Nancy shared the stress that inevitably comes with tying balloons, picking a deejay, hanging streamers, and positioning oneself in the hallway at school in order to cross paths with you-know-who. I don't think it showed, but as the weeks wore on I became increasingly impatient with Nancy and thought: *Give me a break! It's just a prom, Nancy. There is life after this dance. Why don't you just plan to go with your friends and quit this monotonous worrying, for God's sake!*

I often lay adult expectations on young people I work with, thinking that they should be able to keep everything in long-range perspective. But teenagers, for the most part, live in the present. What matters most for young people is what is happening right now. How their parents are treating them, how their peers are responding to them, and what might happen for them today or this week really mean just about everything.

Seeing the big picture, considering their lives as "in process," is difficult for teenagers, perhaps beyond the capacity of many. Because of this, it is important for me as a minister to young people to live with them in the present. For most young people, the zit on their nose, the rejection of that guy or girl, or who they are seen with walking to school are foremost concerns. As much as I would like to, I cannot dismiss these concerns as petty or insignificant. What matters to them should matter to me. If I can live with them in all of their anxieties, even those anxieties that seem silly to me, I may be able to lead them into some of the larger issues of life.

For me, this perspective on ministry derives from a theology of the Incarnation. I believe that living with people where they are at is precisely what God has done in Jesus. Jesus did not cling to his prerogatives as God, but emptied himself, seeking solidarity with humanity by becoming one of us. What an incredible mystery! There is no better model for ministry than the one God chose: the Incarnation.

The best youth work happens when adults seek real solidarity with young people. This does not mean that I have to behave like a teenager or that I look for artificial ways to impress young people, but that I enter their world in compassion as an adult friend.

This is risky business because it means that I can no longer cling to my prerogatives as an adult. I must be willing to leave the company and comfort of my adult world. I must be willing to serve youth, to let go of the accepted order of things where adults are somehow dominant. This involves leaving my comfortable kitchen or office and physically entering into their world, messy though it may be. Anyone who has made this a regular part of their youth ministry knows how vulnerable and outright terrifying such a move can be and has, perhaps, faintly tasted the risk God takes for us in the Incarnation.

Meditation

Let the same mind be in you that was in Christ Jesus,
    who, though he was in the form of God,
        did not regard equality with God
        as something to be exploited,
    but emptied himself,
        taking the form of a slave,
        being born in human likeness.
    And being found in human form,
        he humbled himself
        and became obedient to the point of death—
        even death on a cross.
    Therefore God also highly exalted him
        and gave him the name
        that is above every name,

> so that at the name of Jesus
>   every knee should bend,
>   in heaven and on earth and under the earth,
> and every tongue should confess
>   that Jesus Christ is Lord,
>   to the glory of God the Father.
>
> (Phil. 2:5–11, NRSV)

Reflection

What attitudes and anxieties of young people are the hardest for me to accept? Has there been a time, recently, when my expectations were too "adult" for them?

Prayer

Lord Jesus Christ, you were willing to surrender all that was rightly yours as God in order to make yourself available to me. Thank you for making yourself known, for sharing in the messy business of humanity. I know that there was risk in that move, in that act of love. Give me the courage to take this risk for the young people in my life. Help me to be sensitive to what kids care about, to take them seriously in all that they are experiencing. Show me how I can, with patience, lead them to places beyond, places where they can see you and the many others who need your love in our world. Amen.

❖ 18 ❖
Disturbed by Honesty:
When Kids Reveal Themselves

Today at a pool party, Neil, one of the guys in our youth group, made a casual comment that startled me. He was talking about a party that took place the previous weekend. As he recounted the night, he nonchalantly informed me that he had been sick for two days following the party due to alcohol poisoning. Knowing Neil, I was not surprised by what had happened to him, but I was surprised by his complete honesty with me.

As I reflect on it now, I realize how humorous my initial, internal response to Neil's candid account was: *Why are you telling me this? I am your youth minister, you idiot. You're not supposed to tell me things like that. You're supposed to be good!*

I sometimes cannot believe how surprised and uncomfortable I feel when a young person reveals something "steamy," with no apparent remorse. My conversation with Neil today reminded me of an experience that a friend of mine in youth work had a few years ago. He had taken a group of young people away for a weekend at a nearby camp. After they returned home from the weekend, the director of the camp called to complain that he had found beer cans in the woods. He chided my friend for not doing a better job of screening the young people he brought to a Christian camp and informed him that if he would like to come back in the future, he should bring better-behaved young people.

My friend said that at first he felt embarrassed about the situation and disappointed that he had not been in better control of what the kids were doing. He also felt hurt and taken advantage of, and he wondered if the weekend had been worth it. But on further reflection he realized that there were no better kids to invest a weekend with! So maybe his kids weren't a really morally upright bunch. Still, he had gotten them to come away for a whole weekend on a "religious thing." Perhaps it was a sign that he'd been doing something right.

The discomfort I felt with Neil's honesty forces me to re-evaluate what it is I am looking for in my relationships with young people and to question how open I am to the sometimes disappointing realities of their lives. I confess that there is a need in me to know that I am doing something right, that I am having an impact, and that the young people I am involved with are maturing in their relationship with Jesus and his church. Hearing and experiencing the rough edges in kids' lives, especially firsthand, can cause me to wonder: *Gee, where are all the wonderful things happening in your life as a result of my influence?* But I am afraid that if kids pick up this attitude, they will simply resort to wearing a "Sunday-school face" when they are around me. I know I don't want that.

I am not exactly sure why Neil told me about his episode of intoxication. I don't know if he was crying out for help or if he was just bragging, thinking I might be impressed by his adventure. I know that I was uncomfortable hearing his story and did not really know how to respond. I was stuck somewhere between wanting to be a cool adult in his eyes and, at the same time, wanting to express my disapproval.

My internal reaction to Neil's openness about getting drunk suggests that I am not as open to some of the negative realities in kids' lives as I want to be. I am thankful to God that in spite of this, at least some of the kids I know feel that they can be honest with me without being condemned.

Meditation

"The Son of Man came eating and drinking and they said, 'Look, he is a glutton and a drunkard, a friend of tax collectors and sinners. . . .'" (Matt. 11:19, NAB)

Reflection

Are the kids I work with able to be honest with me about their moral failings? Am I doing anything to inhibit this kind of honesty in my relationships with young people?

Prayer

Lord, sometimes when a young person shares or does something messy, it makes me uncomfortable because I am not sure how to respond. Help me to accept kids where they are at and not where I think they should be.

Thank you for the times when a kid startles me back into a

realization of what kind of friend I want to be to the young people I work with.

Jesus, help me to find that balance in compassion where I neither condone irresponsible behavior nor condemn the person confiding in me. Help me, Lord, to be a good steward of the relationships that you have entrusted to me. Amen.

◆ 19 ◆

Let's Rock!
Listening to the Music Our Kids Love

A good friend of mine named Kevin recently told me about a rock concert he had been to with a group of young people from a local parish. He had been asked to come along as a chaperone by a friend who coordinated some of the youth activities. Having little responsibility and a free ticket, Kevin went, looking forward to having a good time.

As the concert began, he realized how unexcited the adults were about being there. One of them pulled out earplugs and stuffed them in her ears so that she would not have to listen to the music. Another had brought a book along and stayed in the car, reading. Of all the adult leaders, Kevin, who is not a member of the youth group's parish, was the only one who sat and listened to the entire concert with the young people.

The two of us laughed together as he recounted how overtly miserable the adults were during this rock concert. While the young people talked excitedly about the music after the show, the adults could not wait to get home.

Music is sacred to all of us. Music, our own or others', speaks to our heart in a language all its own. Of all the arts, music clearly appeals most directly and effectively to the hearts of young people. I recently heard a speaker tell a group of youth workers that the spirituality of young people in the nineties will be increasingly rooted in music. It certainly is true that music speaks to and for many young people for many different reasons, with many different consequences.

I enjoy many kinds of music: rock, classical, blues, big band, folk, contemporary Christian, Gregorian chant, rap. Depending on the day and the mood, you could find me listening to just about anything. I love music because I am a human being. But I do not like all music. Some music that is loved by young people I do not like at all. This is nothing new. As a teenager I loved and played loud music that drove my parents crazy, and I fully expect that my own children will pay me back for this some day.

I know of some adults in the church who believe that secular rock and rap music is the single most destructive force at work in the lives of our youth. I sat in one seminar for youth ministers recently where the speaker advocated ridiculing the musical heroes of young people if they represent a message antithetical to the Christian Gospel. He spoke proudly of ripping down posters of Madonna and Michael Jackson in his own child's bedroom.

I'm not comfortable with that approach. I am not sure that our task is to go head-to-head in battle with secular rock and pop music. For one thing, it would be hypocritical of me, since I happen to enjoy the music of many contemporary secular rock musicians. Aside from that, I am just not ready to make those kinds of decisions for my young friends, assuming they would even let me do so in the first place.

On the other hand, I am not naive. I don't doubt for a minute that much of what is churned out by the rock 'n' roll industry—the music, the images, and the lifestyles—has a destructive impact on the young people I know. I am annoyed, frustrated, and often angered by what I hear and see being marketed to young people by the music industry.

Rather than ridicule the musicians or wage war against their music, I believe my primary role as a minister to youth is to equip them with the skills necessary for discerning and challenging the values the music contains. I decided long ago that I was not going to presume that my chief gift to young people was to provide them with answers. Instead, I think the best thing I can hope to do, the thing that will last long after I am gone from their lives, is to help young people develop an ability to distinguish between what is true and what is false. I am much more interested in seeing young people grow in their ability to look at things critically than I am in telling them how they should think or feel about certain things.

Practically speaking, this means I have to be willing to listen to the music that is important to the young people I work with. If I sit and listen to 2 Live Crew or Guns n' Roses with young people, as painful as that can be, I just might have a chance to dialog with them about the music. If I put earplugs in, rip down the posters, or ridicule the musicians, I'll be tuned out before the discussion ever begins.

Meditation

Although I am free in regard to all, I have made myself a slave to all so as to win over as many as possible. To the Jews I became like a Jew to win over Jews. . . . To those

outside the law I became like one outside the law
. . . to win over those outside the law. To the weak I
became weak, to win over the weak. I have become all
things to all, to save at least some. All this I do for the sake
of the gospel, so that I too may have a share in it. (1 Cor.
9:19–23, NAB)

Reflection

What music is important to me? Am I as discerning in my
choice of music as I hope young people will be in theirs?

Prayer

Lord God, thank you for the power and mystery of music. I
know that eternity will be filled with beautiful music: music to
express praise and glory and honor to you, spontaneous music
to express joy, peace, and liberation. And I pray with confidence
that it won't be all "church music."

Lord, like all of your good gifts, music is sometimes distort-
ed to the point where it becomes a destructive force in our life.
Help me to be a discriminating listener of both my music and
the music that young people listen to, so that I might model to
them a way of critical discernment in their music choices.
Amen.

❖ 20 ❖
Learning from Others:
An Invitation to Shut Up

Last evening I was involved with a retreat for youth at a parish north of the city. The nice thing about the evening was that I had no real responsibility for anything that was going to take place. I was going as a diocesan representative simply to support the retreat team, to see friends from the parishes, and to personally take part in the experience.

One of the retreat activities called for the young people to break into small groups and for the small group of adult leaders present also to meet as a group. The ten of us in the adult group had no set agenda beyond getting acquainted and describing our various ministries. I think the retreat team was just trying to keep us out of trouble.

As is often the case in situations like this, our group encountered a substantial period of silence once the introductions were completed and we were on our own. As each silent second ticked by, I became increasingly anxious about what was—or was not—taking place. I felt the urge to speak up in order to get the ball rolling, but I wasn't sure what to say. As glances were thrown my way, I perceived that a few in the group were looking to me to be a facilitator because of my diocesan position. Everything within me wanted to oblige them by moving us out of the silence and into the comfort of talk: away from risk, vulnerability, and uncertainty, and into the safe haven of talk. Against all odds, I kept my mouth shut.

When someone finally did speak up, I sensed a sudden relaxation in the group members. Our conversation progressed through topics such as alcohol abuse, discipline within youth meetings, and the importance of building relationships of trust with young people. My usual tendency in a group discussion like this one is to enter right in with my own opinions and stories, to actively seek solutions to problems as they are presented, and to generally share my comprehensive wisdom, whatever the topic.

Throughout this conversation, however, I had a persistent inner dialog running. Each time a question was raised within the group, such as, "What do you do when . . . " I felt an immediate temptation to offer a solution. At the same time I felt that temptation, however, I felt an overpowering directive within me saying *shut up!* This inner call to remain silent was unyielding throughout the evening, and its persistence took me by surprise. Many times I felt I had something valuable to say or something helpful to teach, but this only strengthened the antagonist arguing inside me: *Is it really important that you add this to the conversation? Is it important to anyone besides you? Are you being asked to teach something here? Do you really believe that this conversation needs your insight?*

Lately I have been thinking a great deal about the little proverb that goes something like this: "I never learned anything from talking." This is a hard lesson for me, prolific talker that I am. Yet it is an important discipline and principle for me to learn. My inclination in ministry is to believe that what I know or what I have experienced is what others need, and it is my role to share it with them at every opportunity.

I think I am learning, however slowly, to be quiet more often. It is taking a long time, but I am discovering the joy— although it is sometimes *quite* difficult—of remaining silent and letting others uncover the truth. Increasingly I am embracing those clumsy silences and resisting the temptation to shower young people with my valuable insights. I am recognizing that at times I should offer nothing, trusting in the sure knowledge that the truth is much larger than me and will emerge from others, for my benefit as well as that of the young people I work with.

Oh, yeah—and I'm beginning to learn some new things.

Meditation

It was said about Abba Agathon that for three years he carried a pebble around in his mouth until he learned to be silent. (Yushi Nomura, *Desert Wisdom*, p. 5)

Reflection

How easy is it for me to choose to remain quiet when I have an insight to share?

Prayer

Jesus, at times your silence loudly spoke the truth. When the religious leaders brought to you the woman caught in adultery, you did not argue with them but were silent. When you were confronted, you stood mute before your accusers so that they could hear themselves. You knew when to speak and when to remain silent.

Lord, I love the sound of my own voice too much! Continue to teach me to be silent more often and to listen to others more. Let me be a good steward of my words, discerning what is necessary and what is not—before I open my mouth. And in my silence, open up my ears to hear the many things you have been wanting to teach me for so long. Amen.

❖ 21 ❖

From Fear to Love:
Risking a Simple Hello

Last Saturday my wife, Sue, and I rode to the park on our bicycles, toting our two boys. It was one of those first, beautiful, sunny, and warm days of spring, and we had nothing to do but play together as a family. After a leisurely spell at the park, we loaded our boys back onto the bikes and prepared to continue our ride.

As we did this, I noticed three young men playing basketball on the court nearby. One of them was a guy named Brian who had graduated from our local high school two years ago and was now a sophomore at a nearby college. My contact with Brian while he was in high school had been mostly unpleasant.

Brian had always been one of the largest guys in his class, and he was subjected to the mockery that often comes with being extra big. To compensate, he became involved in both football and basketball. Finding his size to be an advantage in sports, he began to use it to his advantage outside of sports, often intimidating those smaller than himself. The very bigness that made Brian the object of mockery in his younger years became his greatest strength during his last years of high school. He fancied himself to be a real tough guy, and the image was effective. His response to me—an adult connected to "churchy" or "God things"—had always been cold.

Since I had not seen Brian for a few years, I debated whether to say hello to him. My initial inclination was to ride by him without saying anything. Why not? He probably wouldn't notice me, and besides, I didn't feel like being blown off by him. I could see myself riding over to say hello only to have Brian kind of smirk and say, "Oh, hi," without interrupting his basketball play.

So I started to ride by without saying anything to him. But almost immediately I stopped my bicycle and thought: *Wait a minute! What is your problem, Dan? Are you afraid to say hello to this guy because he might ignore you? Are you going to let your petty fears dictate how you respond to everybody? So what if he does reject you. That's his problem. Get your butt back over there and say hello!*

While my wife and boys waited patiently, I rode back over to the basketball court and said hello to Brian. Immediately his face lit up, and he responded with surprising enthusiasm and warmth. We talked for about five minutes about his school, my children, and some mutual friends. I was impressed with how well he seemed to be doing.

It was a little thing, saying hello to a guy shooting baskets. Yet as I rode away, I recognized that little thing as a personal victory. So often I find that I respond to people and situations out of fear rather than out of love. Instead of just riding away, which I could have done easily, this time I risked a hello. I never expected the warm reaction I received from Brian; that was a bonus. What feels even better is knowing that this time my response was not dictated by fear but rather by a renewed confidence in the strength of Christ's love.

Meditation

> In love there is no room for fear,
> but perfect love drives out fear,
> because fear implies punishment
> and whoever is afraid has not come to perfection in love.
> Let us love, then,
> because he first loved us.
>
> (1 John 4:18–19, NJB)

Reflection

When does the fear of rejection limit or paralyze me in my youth work? With whom might Jesus be calling me to risk more for the sake of his love?

Prayer

Lord Jesus, you know how often my actions are motivated by fear rather than by selfless love. You know how hard it is for me to risk when there is the chance that I will be ignored or rejected.

Thank you for the taste of small victories. Give me courage, Lord, to take greater risks in my relationships and to trust confidently in the affirmation of your love. Amen.

❖ 22 ❖
A Night on the Town: Enjoying Real Friendship with Young People

Each Tuesday I gather with eleven young people for prayer, Bible study, and pizza—not necessarily in that order. I am especially close to two of the guys in this group, Mike and Chet, because of a summer trip we took together.

Mike and Chet are really fun to be around. While it is true that I am married, a father, and more than a decade older than they are, the friendship I have with these two seventeen-year-old seniors means a great deal to me. In fact, I would say that I probably laugh more on a regular basis with these two than I do with anyone else, outside of my family, at this time in my life.

Last Saturday we decided that we would make a night of it. I don't get to do this informal socializing with young people as often as I used to, so I was looking forward to our time out together. We made plans to go to a movie, and I was to drive.

When Mike and I arrived, Chet came out of his house dressed in a dark gray tuxedo that was at least two sizes too small and looked like it was made in 1955. As Mike and I laughed hysterically, Chet just stood there with a big grin.

"Why are you dressed in that?" I asked after regaining my composure.

"I found it in the attic. We're going to the movies, right?" With this, Chet pulled out a big flashlight, and I realized that I had just picked up the theater "usher."

On the way to the movie, Chet came up with another idea. Since it was prom season, he suggested that we pull up to a house and he would pretend that he was arriving to pick up his date for the dance. I would play "dad" out in the car while he went to the front door to ask if "Jane" was ready to go.

Now, a serious youth leader who understands his responsibility to the church and to the community would have, of course, derailed this silliness well before it could take place. But I thought it was just about the best idea I had ever heard, and when I finally stopped laughing, we tucked Mike away in the back seat and pulled into a driveway.

While I sat up as high as possible in the driver's seat, letting go with deep coughs every so often, Chet positioned himself on the front step, gave one last thumbs-up toward the car, and rang the doorbell. As the door opened, a couple who looked to be in their fifties emerged.

"Hello, Mr. and Mrs. Schwartz? I'm Chet. I've come to pick up Jane for the dance!" Big grin.

The looks on the faces of this couple were priceless. As they tried to sympathetically explain to Chet that he had the wrong house, it was apparent that they were biting their lips to keep from bursting out laughing. Chet played his part beautifully. As we drove away, waving to the couple, I wondered who, the couple or us, would have the most fun talking about it for the rest of the night.

At the movies, Chet stationed himself just inside the door of the theater. It was one of those typical suburban, eight-screen mega-theaters where you never find real ushers. As people entered the darkened room, they were startled by Chet's flash-light and his request to see their tickets. To their amusement, and sometimes great pleasure—he received offers of tips—he walked them down to their seats with great fanfare and flashing of lights. At one point a middle-aged couple requested that Chet ask a group of young girls a few rows back to keep their noise level down. Mike and I were practically howling as Chet approached these girls and, with great seriousness, informed them that they would have to be quiet "out of consideration to the other patrons of our theater."

What a fun night! That night helps me to realize again that the relationships I have with high school kids are not one-way relationships. We speak so often of the need to build friendships with young people so that our ministry with them will be fruitful. But my night out with Chet and Mike reminds me of how much *I* get out of these friendships. Chet and Mike are not simply projects in my ministry but friends who are truly impor-tant to me. Just as surely as I have something to offer them, they are giving me as much back—gifts of laughter, vulnerabili-ty as they share their struggles with surprising candor, and free spirits that know how to have fun; gifts that many adults, like me, too often forget how to share.

Meditation

If ever our world needed jesters, it is now. We have forgotten how to relax, how to laugh, how to play. We have forgotten how to be. In our world today, laughter can be a sign of deep faith, deep love, and deep hope. It may be our highest manifestation of compassion. (Tessa Bielecki, in Susan Walker, ed., *Speaking of Silence,* p. 244)

Reflection

Which young persons in my life right now can I genuinely have fun with? What kinds of opportunities exist for having fun with young friends?

Prayer

God, thank you for the young people you have brought into my life who have ministered to me in sometimes unexpected ways. I am seeing more and more that my commitment to building authentic friendships with young people involves being open to the ways they can touch and heal my life, and not simply to the ways I can help them.

Open my eyes, Lord, to the many gifts you give me through these friendships. And protect me (dear God!) from the disease of becoming a "serious" person. Amen.

Part 4

◆

GRACE

23

My Haircut:
Taking Jesus to the Barbershop

This morning I went to get my hair cut. I often go to this particular shop because basically it is the cheapest place in town; my hair is pretty straightforward, and I figure scissors are scissors. The shop opens at nine o'clock, and I got there just a few minutes after it opened.

When I arrived, a woman was in the shop getting things in order for the day. She didn't acknowledge me when I came in, so I waited patiently because I knew that she knew I was standing there. When she finally came to the reception counter, she picked up a pen, grabbed a pad of paper, and mumbled something to me that I couldn't hear.

"I beg your pardon?" I asked.

"Name?" she asked, this time with great force. After regaining my balance, I told her my name, and as she turned and walked away she said, "This way!"

So now I'm thinking: *Okay, welcome to Nazi-Cuts. This woman is going to hold a scissors to my head in just a few seconds.* I seriously thought of saying "never mind" and walking out, but I sat down obediently, and she strapped that white cloth collar around my neck just a little bit tighter than I had ever felt it before.

For the next fifteen minutes she didn't say a word to me. I watched her in the big mirror I was sitting in front of, and it seemed pretty clear that she was angry, uptight, and unhappy. Since we were the only ones in the shop, I guessed that someone had called in sick or to say that they were going to be late, and this woman was not happy about running the shop all by herself. I began to try to imagine what her life was like. She looked to be in her forties. Her face showed evidence that she was under a lot of stress; she looked tired. While I studied her, I also began to hear myself thinking: *I don't deserve this treatment. I can't believe how rude this woman is being!*

I usually give the standard one- or two-dollar tip to a haircutter. They have a glass jar stuffed with dollar bills right there on the counter in front of the mirror for you to look at while you are getting clipped. But today I thought: *No way!* I formulated a response: *Look, if you expect me to tip you after the*

*way you have treated me, you must be kidding! I don't know what's
eating you this morning, but you can't take it out on me and then
expect me to tip you! Ha!*

I was ready. I was determined—at least for about three
minutes. Then another thought hit me: *Wait a minute. Here you
are strategizing about how you are going to get even with this woman
when you can tell that she is obviously very unhappy. That's a real
neat Christian response! Why don't you try acting like the disciple of
Jesus you claim to be? Engage this poor woman in some conversation! Try to say something that might cheer her up, for God's sake!*

I was inwardly embarrassed by my initial reaction. The
Holy Spirit was definitely kicking some butt. Eventually I began
to engage the woman in a simple conversation about a report
the radio station was broadcasting, her children, the new job
she was waiting to hear about. After a bit of this, the tension in
her face seemed to ease a little. By the time I left we were saying
things like "thanks a lot" and "have a good weekend"; nothing
earth-shattering, but a heck of a lot nicer than what either of us
was experiencing fifteen minutes earlier. Oh, and it did cost me
a buck.

This encounter has been sticking with me all day. I am
realizing how easy it is for me to be a Christian witness when I
am in a well-defined ministry situation: spending time with
young people, speaking to a group, training volunteers, meeting
with pastors, or working on a program. I pray before these
times, at least sometimes. I prepare. I consciously ask: How can
I be good news in this situation? How can my life or words
reflect my commitment to Jesus?

But get me on Route 128—where I spend an hour every
weekday—and watch out. I make faces at people, mutter unedi-
fying things about them, and maneuver my car in such a
manner that if anyone were videotaping me, they could probably discredit my ministry in a minute.

Today's haircut situation provides a renewed challenge for
me. Can I bring the same intensity and intentional effort that I
put into official ministry into my daily encounters with people:
Driving in traffic? Standing in line at the grocery store? Talking
to the mail carrier? Places where I am not necessarily expected
to behave like a Christian? Places where I really find out what
kind of a Christian I am.

Meditation

Not only does the love of God have attention for its substance; the love of our neighbor, which we know to be the same love, is made of this same substance. Those who are unhappy have no need for anything in this world but people capable of giving them their attention. The capacity to give one's attention to a sufferer is a very rare and difficult thing; it is almost a miracle; it *is* a miracle. Nearly all those who think they have this capacity do not possess it. Warmth of heart, impulsiveness, pity are not enough. (Simone Weil, *Waiting for God*, p. 114)

Reflection

Where or when is it hardest for me to act like a Christian? Are there persons that I casually meet for whom I could be good news if I were more intentional about it?

Prayer

Jesus, I am aware that I can be intentional about my Christian witness when I am in ministry situations but that I hardly give it any thought when I am at the doctor's office or in the grocery store.

I realize that you call me to something greater. Wake me up to the many needs and many opportunities for witnessing that I encounter each day. Show me how I can bring good news, even at the barbershop. Amen.

24

The House Is Burning!
Longing to Be a Hero

This morning, after a particularly hard night with one of our two little boys, our phone rang at seven o'clock. I really don't appreciate phone calls that early. I was already up, getting ready for an all-day diocesan meeting, but my wife and kids were still asleep, and I wanted to keep it that way. Phones seem to ring louder at that hour, so I picked it up quickly, irritated and wanting to find out who the jerk was, calling at that time of day.

It was Nick. Nick is seventeen and has been a friend for about two years. He has been known to do some crazy things—especially to me—and now I wondered what he was up to.

"You sound tired. Did I wake you up?"

"No."

"Is it too early to call?"

"Yes, Nick."

Nick's family is from India, and they remain very committed to their heritage. His father, a devout Hindu, died just about the time I met Nick. Nick is extremely bright and serious about living a moral life. He and I have had numerous discussions about what he believes in and who Jesus is in my life.

"My mother dropped me off at school and just called from work—she's freaking out! She thinks she left some incense burning at home on her altar and is afraid the house might burn down."

"What?"

"Can you go to our house, check my mother's altar, and make sure nothing is burning?"

On my way to Nick's house, I thought about the fact that this was the first time I had been asked to rescue a Hindu altar. Do other youth ministers do this often?

My imagination ran wild as I drove to the potentially burning house. Will I beat the fire engines? Is the dog on fire? I could see the headlines in tomorrow's paper:

Local Youth Worker Injured Slightly in Parakeet Rescue
or
Hero Battles Flames, Saves Rare Stamp Collection

But nothing was burning when I got to Nick's house, not even the incense. Of course I was relieved, but the relief was mixed with a strange sense of disappointment. How many chances will I get to rescue a home from flames at 7:00 a.m.? If only I could have stamped out a smouldering rug or actually operated one of those small, red fire extinguishers.

It is easy for me to think sometimes that my life is not exciting enough: times when I feel that my life is not what it could be, times when things that I usually enjoy and find meaningful seem small and insignificant. Where is the sensational? Where is the excitement? Where is the unusual? Is this all there is?

Then I watch my three-year-old son as he attempts to rake the yard. I watch my one-year-old eat a Popsicle. I smell the coming autumn in the warm evening breeze as I walk with my wife, a friend who is always willing to go for a walk in the evening. And I remember that someone once said, "Mediocrity is very underrated."

Meditation

We do not need to carry out grand things in order to show a great love for God and for our neighbor. It is the intensity of love we put into our gestures that makes them into something beautiful for God. (Mother Teresa, *Heart of Joy*, p. 116)

Reflection

Are my eyes able to see the sacred in the ordinary hours of my life? How is God blessing me today?

Prayer

Lord, I am sometimes tempted to think that my life is not exciting enough, that I need something dramatic to come along and offer me the possibility of being a hero.

Help me to recognize all the opportunities to truly be a hero in this life you have blessed me with. Let the little things I do today be filled with an intense, heroic love. Amen.

❖ 25 ❖
Corpus Christi:
At Home in the Body of Christ

I have never claimed to be a mystic. I am usually in awe when I read the writings of those whose vision and experience of God's love have taken them to depths that almost defy description. My daily life with Jesus has been, for the most part, nonecstatic. Occasionally, however, I will experience an unexpected revelation. It usually comes like a dawning, as if a fog has lifted before my sleepy eyes to uncover a beautiful hillside that has been there all along.

Sunday, on the feast of Corpus Christi, which also happens to be the name of our parish, I had one of those revelatory experiences. Excitement filled the air that day, because the parish community was going to have a picnic on the church lawn after Mass. During the liturgy, as I made my way forward to the altar to receive the Eucharist, I suddenly became aware of all those around me who were also coming forward for communion. Unexpectedly, I found myself wanting to look deeply into their faces: the middle-aged woman with a tired-looking face, the old man across from me, slightly hunched over and moving with difficulty. I was struck by the immensity of life embodied in the people who surrounded me and processed with me: some young, some old; some rich, some poor; some whole, some broken; some beautiful, some unseemly. All with a history. All on a journey. I couldn't take my eyes off of them.

I suddenly found myself overwhelmed by the sense that I was connected to these people, to these lives. More than as a mere participant in the eucharistic liturgy, I saw my life—in all of its complexity—as a part of something much larger. I was seized by a deepened understanding that I was, with these others, the body and blood of Christ, living, breathing, hoping, joyful, and sorrowful.

As I knelt, back in the pew, I found myself awed by this revelation of the body and blood of Jesus and the realization that nothing in my life was complete outside of my relationship to Jesus as a member of his body and blood. Every part of my life as I understand it—my loves, my hates, my hopes, my failures, my brokenness, my history, my future—finally finds its home in belonging to Jesus. Apart from this, nothing makes sense. Nothing else gives life; nothing else sustains hope. I had a new sense of how I share this profound dependence on the gift of Jesus' body and blood in the Eucharist with the many others around me who bring their own unique life to this place each week, even each day, to offer it with Jesus as a sacrifice.

What keeps me alive in youth work? Why do I do what I do, and how can I keep doing it? Where can I go to make sense of it all? I don't know how other people in youth ministry answer these questions. Even as I grow in the realization of my need to see my whole life rooted in the mystery and celebration of the Eucharist, I don't find it any easier to communicate that understanding to others.

As I grow older, I find myself wanting to go to Mass more often. I used to think that the elderly went to Mass every day because they had nothing else to do with their mornings. That's what I used to think.

Meditation

> Mrs. Broadwater said when she was a child and received the Host, she thought of it as the Holy Ghost, He being the "most portable" person of the Trinity; now she thought of it as a symbol and implied that it was a pretty good one. I then said, in a very shaky voice, "Well, if it's a symbol, to hell with it." That was all the defense I was capable of but I realize now that this is all I will ever be able to say about it, . . . except that it is the center of existence for me; all the rest of life is expendable. (Flannery O'Connor, *Collected Works,* p. 977)

Reflection

Where is my spiritual home? Where do I go with my hopes, failures, dreams, confusion, joy, anxieties, and loneliness . . . to make sense of it all?

Prayer

> Soul of Christ, make me holy.
> Body of Christ, be my salvation.
> Blood of Christ, let me drink your wine.

Water flowing from the side of Christ, wash me clean.
Passion of Christ, strengthen me.
Kind Jesus, hear my prayer;
hide me within your wounds
and keep me close to you.
Defend me from the evil enemy.
Call me at my death
to the fellowship of your saints,
that I may sing your praise with them
through all eternity. Amen.

(Prayer to our Redeemer, in
Prayers Before and After Mass [The Roman Missal], p. 6)

❖ 26 ❖

Busted!
Freedom to Laugh at Myself

During my first year as a staff worker for Young Life, a friend of mine told me about a fun thing her group members were doing. They would go to a young person's home at about 6:30 a.m. on a school morning to tape a surprise wake-up with a video camera. The next week they would show this video at their meeting. It quickly became the talk of the high school and even increased attendance at the group meeting because kids were dying to see who had been captured on video that week. Immediately recognizing what a great idea this was, I naturally did what every good youth minister does: I stole it.

For several months I ran the "Morning Wake-Up Service," capturing on film, each week, the morning routine of one lucky high schooler from the moment of waking, or rather, being awakened, to his or her arrival at school. It was definitely a hit. Each week I would call parents to enlist their cooperation, and each week different kids would worry—or in some cases, hope—that they would be next.

In the midst of all of this, unknown to me, a handful of young people were plotting revenge. They found an opportunity to even the score when they learned that I had taken measures to avoid encountering a police officer who was parked on a side street when I went by, exceeding—not much—the speed limit. I hadn't liked the expression on his face when our eyes met, so after quickly disappearing from his sight around a bend in the road, I made one or two extra turns onto roads I had not been planning to travel that morning.

Several days later, when my doorbell rang, I opened the door to see a police officer on my step and a police cruiser in the driveway with the blue lights flashing.

"Mr. Ponsetto?"

"Ah, yes?"

"I am Officer Peterson, and I have a summons here for you to appear in the Waltham District Court next Tuesday morning at 9:00 a.m."

"What? What are you talking about? Why am I being summoned to appear in court?"

"Well, Mr. Ponsetto, it says here that you eluded a police

officer on Route 27 to avoid a speeding ticket. Could you come out to the car for a few moments so that I can ask you a few questions?"

Gulp. So it was true; that cop was after me! How did he get my license number? I couldn't believe this was happening to me, and I kept thinking what a hassle it was going to be to have to appear in court. I walked out to the cruiser, groaning and trying, with great animation, to explain my innocence.

Just as we reached the car, two young people came running around the corner, laughing and "high-fiving" each other, calling me a sucker. Still perplexed, I looked at the officer, who was now grinning widely and unclipping a small microphone from his uniform. Two more kids called out from a second-story window next door, from where they had captured the entire scene on video.

Actually, my wife had related the incident when the kids came looking for some dirt on me, and they had recruited one of their favorite police officers to help them with their plan.

I had really been taken in by their scheme. While they all laughed and did a little victory dance around me, I just stood there, first relieved, then embarrassed, and finally, doubled over in laughter. That was, without question, one of the funniest, best-organized things a group of young people has ever done to me. Obviously there was no morning wake-up video shown at the meeting that next week, but everyone had a good laugh at my expense.

One of the most important things I have learned from my best mentors is how important it is to be able to laugh at myself. I am convinced that this ability to take myself lightly is a spiritual virtue, one to be nurtured. I hope that laughing at myself—not just when people play jokes on me but also when I embarrass myself, make mistakes, or fail in some way—is a sign that I have tasted something of the mercy of God. Certainly it is a sign that I am beginning to understand who I am in God's eyes, for God most definitely laughs hard and often at me and invites me in on the fun.

Meditation

Not everybody has a sense of humor. That calls for an altruistic detachment from oneself and a mysterious sympathy with others which is felt even before they open their mouths. . . . A good laugh is a sign of love; it may be said to give us a glimpse of, or a first lesson in, the love that God bears for every one of us. . . . God laughs, says the Bible. When the last piece of human folly makes the last burst of human laughter ring out crisp and clear in a doomed world, is it too much to imagine that this laugh will resemble that of God . . . and seem to convey that, in spite of everything, all's well? (Karl Rahner, quoted in Charles Reutemann, *Let's Pray/2*, p. 89)

Reflection

How easy is it for me to laugh at myself? When or where do I tend to take myself too seriously?

Prayer

Dear God, you who created humor and gave us the grace to laugh, help me to grow in my ability to laugh at myself. Thank you for allowing me to find forgiveness and healing in the times that we have laughed together. Amen.

My Way or the Highway: Learning to Be Flexible

Recently a young woman named Linda became a volunteer on our leadership team. I have known Linda for many years. She was a member of the Young Life group I volunteered with during my college years in Ann Arbor, and she has now come to Boston to study law. One of the fun things about being reconnected with Linda is that she reminds me of stories from years past, stories that have been dormant in my memory.

One of the stories Linda remembers best and likes to retell in front of as many people as possible has to do with a particular youth meeting that took place during her high school years. I was leading a weekly Young Life club, and for several weeks we had staged a kind of "battle of the bands" lip-syncing contest. The week before this particular meeting, we had crowned the winners of the competition, a group of guys that did a very convincing imitation of the Pointer Sisters, and to tell the truth, I was glad the contest was finally over.

After I had arrived at the meeting in question and was getting ready to begin, Linda and a few of her friends came rushing in to announce they were going to do a lip-sync routine of their favorite group, the B-52's, at that evening's meeting. I politely, but firmly, informed them that they would not be doing a lip-sync performance at the meeting since the contest was over and we had a full program planned. After several minutes of begging and pleading, they realized that I was not going to change my mind. Linda stormed outside onto the driveway and refused to come back into the meeting.

You must realize something about me. At times it is very hard for me to alter my agenda and surrender control of a meeting. This was especially true when I was in college. "Excellence" was my motto. Excellence meant being prepared: having guitars perfectly tuned, skits well-rehearsed, and talks polished. Surrendering to spontaneity put that all at risk.

While I held my hard line, Linda continued to sulk out in the driveway, periodically dispatching friends to let me know just how unhappy she was with me. I told them that Linda had no one to be mad at and that she could not simply arrive five minutes before our meeting and expect me to give her and her friends ten minutes of the meeting to lip-sync "Rock Lobster," no matter how long they had practiced. I was sure I was right. The only problem was that I still had four girls mad at me, one supremely mad. That kind of hurt the excellence philosophy I held so dear.

In the end I gave in. I can still remember Linda and her girlfriends leaping back and forth, throwing their heads around to the music of the B-52's, and looking so serious. Looking at her face, you could barely tell that Linda had been crying. I stood on the side, suddenly remembering how important it was in high school to be able to play *my* song, to be able to move to *my* song, and to be able to draw others into *my* song, hoping that they would experience it the way that I did.

Linda and I now tease each other about that night. She reminds me of my stubbornness and insensitivity to four poor high school girls who were, after all, just trying to impress some boys. I remind her of how she pouted in the driveway. I am able to laugh at myself now, remembering how inflexible I was and how convinced too, that God was going to work best through my own tightly prepared schedule.

While I have become much more flexible in my work with young people, the story reminds me of many other areas in my life today where I am still pretty inflexible, still unwilling to surrender control and trust the Spirit, still sure that my way is the right way. I now can see that rigidity and narrowness not only stunt my growth but also prevent a lot of good things from happening for other people.

Meditation

A passionate longing to grow, to be, is what we need. There can be no place for the anemic in spirit, the skeptics, the pessimists, the sad of heart, the weary, the immobilists. Life is ceaseless discovery. Life is movement. (Pierre Teilhard de Chardin, quoted in Reutemann, *Let's Pray/2*, p. 43)

Reflection

Are there times in my work with young people when I tend to be inflexible or immovable? Are there any programs or events that I have designed that I might be taking a little too seriously?

Prayer

Lord, so often I get set in my ways, believing that I've got to keep you packaged in my own safe programs. I am sorry for the times I have not been open to discovering you in new ways, through new people. I am sorry for the times when I imagined that I had you safely in my hip pocket.

God, as I grow older, I have a deepening sense of how much more I need to learn and experience. Through your grace, help me to believe that you can work in many different, and sometimes surprising, ways. Amen.

◆ 28 ◆
A Letter from Rachael:
A Little Affirmation Goes a Long Way

Every so often, God graces me with a chance to reconnect with an "old kid." About six months ago, I had a phone conversation with a young woman who had been in a youth group that I worked with as a volunteer during college—nine hundred miles and ten years distant from here and now. I had not been in contact with Rachael for about eight years, although on occasion I heard reports on her from mutual friends. When I called one of these mutual friends, Rachael unexpectedly answered the phone. We had a fun conversation, but that was about all I expected from it.

Six months later I received a gem of a letter from her. In the letter, Rachael recounted several times that we had spent together: the time our group went to Colorado; the time we saw each other downtown after she and her girlfriend each had half of their hair dyed purple; the one-on-one conversation about her faith that we had over a Coke—little things I had long forgotten. But she had remembered and taken the time to let me know what they meant to her. And then, at the end of her letter: "I just wanted to let you know that you've made an impact in my life through Christ's spirit, without even knowing it, perhaps."

Yahoo! I am not embarrassed to say that I need affirmation like that sometimes. I don't need a lot, but God knows I need some, and it always tends to come at just the right time. I have begun what I call my "affirmation file." In an unmarked file, I keep any little notes or Christmas cards that God sends my way to boost my spirits, just in case a day comes along when I feel especially down about myself or my vocation in youth ministry.

Many people talk about the direct attacks of Satan in very dramatic terms. But in my life and ministry, I find that the most demonic forces I experience are not sensational, but rather, very subtle. One of the chief weapons of Satan is, I believe, the weapon of discouragement. I think it is a common strategy used on youth ministers. For me it usually starts with internal little whispers like these:

Why don't you get a real job?

Why spend time with teenagers . . . what are you, weird?

You're not making any difference in this town!
What are you doing hanging around a high school gym?
So what are you going to do when you're fifty?
Kids don't want to hear about Jesus, you fool!
The demons that pester me always take advantage of my moods and work on distorting my sense of self-worth or the worth of proclaiming the Gospel. Having an affirmation file, no matter how small, reminds me on the darkest days that it is all worth the effort.

Meditation

O LORD, you have probed me and you know me;
　　you know when I sit and when I stand;
　　you understand my thoughts from afar.
My journeys and my rest you scrutinize,
　　with all my ways you are familiar.
. . . .
Truly you have formed my inmost being;
　　you knit me in my mother's womb.
I give you thanks that I am fearfully, wonderfully made;
　　wonderful are your works.

(Ps. 139:1–14, NAB)

Reflection

What surprise affirmations have I received recently? Do I take the time to nurture others with affirmation when opportunities present themselves?

Prayer

Thank you, God, for inspiring others to send the little notes that I have received over the years, notes that mean so much. Thank you for the small ways you minister to me in friends' comments or phone calls.

Help me, Jesus, to become an affirming person to those who have given meaning to my life. Lift me from my laziness, so that I might take the time to show my gratefulness.

Protect me, Holy Spirit, from the abyss of discouragement and self-doubt. Keep me anchored in your love, and help me to recognize—and laugh off—the tricks of the devil.

All glory, honor, and praise to you, Father, Son, and Holy Spirit, on this day and always. Amen.

❖ 29 ❖
Put in My Place:
Learning Something from a Sophomore

A few days ago I was driving in my car with Mike and Orlando, two high school sophomores I have gotten to know in the past year. We were on our way to a nearby high school to watch a basketball game, and we were pretty loose. As usual, Orlando had brought his music with him, and I had obligingly popped the tape into my car stereo. As we came to a stoplight, we saw a well-dressed young man on the corner, sitting on a bench, obviously waiting for the bus or some other form of transportation. As we pulled to a stop, Mike stuck his head out of the window and called out in an attempt to get the man's attention. As soon as he had it, Mike began to harass him.

"Hey! Hey you! Where did you get those shoes? Ha ha ha . . ."

"Hey, your grandmother called and said she can't pick you up; start walking! Ha ha ha . . ."

"Hey, can you tell me what time it is? Huhhhhh? Ha ha ha . . ."

This was not untypical behavior for Mike. I really like him, but sometimes he has trouble discerning what is appropriate. I was really embarrassed, stuck there at the red light, and I laid into him. "Hey, Mike, cool it. Don't be such a jerk! How do you know I don't know that person?"

As we pulled away from the corner, I continued, more gently, to communicate my displeasure to Mike over the way he had mocked the guy. I knew that he was just having fun, but I really felt that he had stepped over the line. I started to educate him on how humor can sometimes be destructive when it is being enjoyed at someone else's expense. Mike defended himself, first by saying he didn't think it bothered the guy, and then by accusing me of the same type of humor.

Of course, I knew that I had never initiated the kind of humor that hurts or embarrasses other people. I agreed that I do horse around a lot in public situations, but I assured him that he was wrong if he thought that I ever did anything like he had just done to the man at the corner. Yes, I sometimes do crazy things in public, but it's me who looks like the fool. I don't ever make others feel uncomfortable while I am having fun.

Mike continued to insist that I often did the same type of thing and accused me of using a double standard. I was sure he was wrong, until Orlando spoke up from the back seat.

"Well, Dan, I don't usually agree with Mike, but he has a point. You do sometimes push the limit with your humor. We were talking about it the other day in school and, well, it's not like you do it all the time, but sometimes you are pretty sarcastic."

We were talking about it the other day in school? Wait a minute . . . what is going on here? This was actually a topic of conversation in the hallway at the high school? All of a sudden it was two against one, and they were being brutally honest. I swallowed hard and had no choice but to accept their judgment, realizing deep down that they were right.

The interesting thing about our candid exchange is that I feel closer to Mike and Orlando now than I did before. Our friendships have deepened, and I think my respect for them has grown as a result of this humbling confrontation. I sense too that their respect for me grew when they saw that I was willing to learn from them.

I sometimes forget that I am not the only teacher in young people's lives. While it was easy enough to try to teach Mike about his obnoxious behavior, what I forget is that sometimes I need to be taught about my own.

Maybe I can learn even more if I can get in on some of those conversations in the school hallways.

Meditation

"Why do you see the speck in your neighbor's eye, but do not notice the log in your own eye? Or how can you say to your neighbor, 'Let me take the speck out of your eye,' while the log is in your own eye? You hypocrite, first take the log out of your own eye, and then you will see clearly to take the speck out of your neighbor's eye." (Matt. 7:3–5, NRSV)

Reflection

Am I aware of how young people perceive me? What can I learn about myself from their perceptions?

Prayer

Thank you, God, for the experience of being put in my place. It is too easy for me to see myself only as the one who helps others to grow; I welcome the times when I am jolted back to an honest look at myself, as painful as that sometimes is.

Lord, you know me better than I know myself. In your mercy, help me to know and accept myself more fully, especially as I see myself through the eyes of others, so that I can grow beyond my own blind spots into the person you want me to be. I make this prayer in the name of Jesus. Amen.

❖ 30 ❖

Sent by Jesus, to Meet Jesus:
A Paradox in Ministry

About six years ago, I made a Cursillo retreat at a Melkite
Catholic retreat house. While on the retreat I met Brother
Thomas Petitte, a dynamic man of faith who has established
Lazarus House, a shelter for the homeless in Lawrence, Mas-
sachusetts. For a few years after I met him, I volunteered some
time at Lazarus House, and on a few occasions I took small
groups of young people with me.

Last month I took Andrew, Liz, and Hilary, three high
school seniors, with me to Lazarus House to help serve dinner. I
was excited about sharing this experience with them because I
had grown to love the ministry of this shelter and because I
believed that it would be a good experience. Like me, Andrew,
Liz, and Hilary are provincially suburban in their orientation, so
they experienced some nervousness and self-consciousness
going into the evening.

The work routine at the shelter consists of setting up the
dining room, putting out some predinner snacks, and preparing
the meal. After serving the meal, the volunteers are encouraged
to sit and eat with the guests. After cleanup, the volunteers have
time to simply socialize with the guests in the television room
or in the dining room.

The house has a beautiful chapel, and we were fortunate to
be there on an evening when they were having a eucharistic
celebration. The liturgy was especially powerful for us as we
sang and gathered around the Lord's table with people who had
experienced a great deal of pain during their life, but who still
remained hopeful.

After Mass we sat with Joe, a forty-eight-year-old man who
easily looked sixty-five, and listened to his story. Joe was an
alcoholic, separated from his wife for many years. He had
walked from downtown Boston to Lawrence that day to get to
Lazarus House, a distance of over thirty miles; no one would
pick him up as he attempted to hitchhike. He talked about the
violence in the city and described how he had spent several
weeks in the hospital recently, after being hit over the head
with a pipe for the pocketful of change in his pants. His head
still throbbed with pain many hours each day. He told us that

he had not eaten since lunch the day before; he had successfully begged enough money to buy a large submarine sandwich for
dinner, but it had been immediately stolen from him by a larger
man, himself homeless, who often preyed on other homeless
people. It was an extraordinarily sad image for me to envision
Joe gathering together the money to buy his favorite sandwich,
only to be robbed and then have to watch as the bully ate his
dinner.

When Joe finished speaking, there was a long silence. Then
Joe, who had been smiling during the entire telling of his story,
leaned close to us, with his eyes twinkling and a finger raised in
the air, and said: "But I never stop praying! I pray every day. I
don't always get to church, but every night, no matter where I
am I say, 'Jesus, Mary, and Joseph, help me, protect me.' I could
be in the back of an abandoned car or under a bridge, but I
always pray. We have to! I believe that God is watching over me
and cares about me. We can't forget that!"

As we drove home from Lazarus House, the four of us
reflected on our experience. The kids talked about the precon-
ceptions they had had going into the evening, and how now
many of those had been shattered. As part of our reflection, we
recalled the words of Matt. 25:31–46, in which Jesus proclaims
that he is to be found among the poor, the lonely, and the
broken persons of our world.

I am particularly struck and challenged by this paradox in
Christian ministry: I see myself called and empowered by Jesus
to journey forth in his name—to represent him in an unbeliev-
ing world. And yet, I usually find that he has preceded me and
is waiting to reveal himself to me in the most unlikely places
and people.

Meditation

> "Then the king will say to those at his right hand, 'Come,
> you that are blessed by my Father, inherit the kingdom
> prepared for you from the foundation of the world; for I
> was hungry and you gave me food, I was thirsty and you
> gave me something to drink, I was a stranger and you
> welcomed me, I was naked and you gave me clothing, I was
> sick and you took care of me, I was in prison and you
> visited me.' Then the righteous will answer him, 'Lord,
> when was it that we saw you hungry and gave you food, or
> thirsty and gave you something to drink? And when was it

that we saw you a stranger and welcomed you, or naked and gave you clothing? And when was it that we saw you sick or in prison and visited you?' And the king will answer them, 'Truly I tell you, just as you did it to one of the least of these who are members of my family, you did it to me.'" (Matt. 25:34–40, NRSV)

Reflection

How has Jesus revealed himself to me among poor people? Who are "the least" among the young people in my community?

Prayer

Brother Jesus, how often I fail to recognize you! How often I fail to receive you when you come to me as a sister or a brother. I am more comfortable with your divinity, more ready to accept you as the victorious Savior. I am often afraid to touch you or look into your eyes when you confront me as a stranger, a prisoner, a malnourished child, or a victim of AIDS. And yet, there you are in the flesh, waiting to receive me, waiting to be loved and waiting to love. There you are, waiting to show me your life and inviting me to share it.

Dear Jesus, open my heart, my arms, and my eyes, so that I might recognize and receive you, especially among the young people in my midst who are suffering the most. Amen.

Acknowledgments (continued)

The scriptural quotations cited as NAB are from the New American Bible with Revised New Testament. Copyright © 1986 by the Confraternity of Christian Doctrine, Washington, DC. Used with permission. All rights reserved.

The scriptural quotations cited as NJB are from the New Jerusalem Bible. Copyright © 1985 by Darton, Longman and Todd, of London, and Doubleday, a division of Bantam, Doubleday, Dell Publishing Group, of New York. Reprinted by permission of the publishers.

The scriptural quotations cited as NRSV are from the New Revised Standard Version of the Bible. Copyright © 1989 by the Division of Christian Education of the National Council of the Churches of Christ in the United States of America. Used with permission.

The meditation on pages 18–19 is from *The Four Loves,* by C. S. Lewis (New York: Harcourt Brace Jovanovich, 1960), page 169. Copyright © 1960 by Helen Joy Lewis and renewed 1988 by Arthur Owen Bayfield. Reprinted by permission of Harper-Collins and Harcourt Brace Jovanovich.

The meditation on pages 21–22 is from *Psalms Anew: In Inclusive Language,* compiled by Nancy Schreck and Maureen Leach (Winona, MN: Saint Mary's Press, 1986). Copyright © 1986 by Saint Mary's Press. All rights reserved.

The meditation on page 25 is from volume 3 of *The Collected Works of St. Teresa of Ávila,* translated by Kieran Kavanaugh and Otilio Rodriguez (Washington, DC: ICS Publications, 1985), page 386. Copyright © 1985 by the Washington Province of Discalced Carmelites. Used with permission.

The meditation on page 30 is from *Reaching Out: The Three Movements of the Spiritual Life,* by Henri J. M. Nouwen (Great Britain: William Collins Sons, 1976), page 78. Copyright © 1975 by Henri J. M. Nouwen.

The meditation on page 33 is from volume 1 of *Peacemaking: Day by Day,* edited by Mary Lou Kownacki (Erie, PA: Pax Christi USA, 1985), page 61. Copyright © 1985 by Pax Christi USA. Used with permission.

The meditation on pages 37–38 is from *Thomas Merton's Struggle with Peacemaking,* by James H. Forest (Erie, PA: Benet Press, 1983), pages 41–42. Copyright © 1983 by James Forest. Used by permission of Pax Christi USA.

The meditation on page 43 is from *Dark Night of the Soul,* by

What People Are Saying . . .

"After having read several 'how-to' books on youth ministry, I find it refreshing and life-giving to encounter a book that speaks first not to my head but to my heart. From my twelve years of facilitating ministry with adolescents, I found myself relating in some way to every story that Dan Ponsetto shared. This book beautifully encourages me to realize that I am not alone in my joys and struggles, while it stimulates me to reflect on the deeper issues I face in ministering to young people and their families." **Patricia Alfeld,** area director, Young Life, Boston

"In *Praying Our Stories,* Dan Ponsetto has opened the book of his own life and ministry and shared honest tales of everyday happenings, graced with the ordinary of our work and lives, as the places where the invitations of God are experienced. There is no shortage of challenge or comfort herein, where the Scriptures meet life. The account of one youth minister's experiences becomes a call to listen to and pray our own stories as we interact with young people, volunteers, staffs, and the events that come to us through our ministry to, with, by, and for youth. This is a book to be read slowly, to be savored. Be warned . . . it may well prompt you to reflection, writing, storytelling, and prayer of your own." **Joanne M. Cahoon,** coordinator, Office of Youth Ministry, Archdiocese of Baltimore

"*Praying Our Stories* provides parish and school youth ministers an opportunity to reflect on how *their* lives affect *their* ministry. While reading these stories, I could not help but think of my own experiences as a parish youth minister and of how I responded. The mixture of personal storytelling, meditations, and questions provides excellent opportunities for reflection on how we take care of our own faith life and how we challenge youth to be gospel in today's world." **Paul K. Henderson,** associate director, NCCB Secretariat for Family, Laity, Women, and Youth, Washington, DC

"In these pages, everyone who ministers to youth will find an invitation to identify and reflect on their own experiences with young people, to apply the Scriptures, and to pray through these experiences. Through his writing, Dan Ponsetto has a special gift that enables us to see and reflect on our own stories and work with young people. *Praying Our Stories* is a wonderful tool to guide youth ministers into the most essential part of ministry—a healthy pattern of bringing young people to prayer before our God." **Rev. Charles C. McCoart, Jr.,** director, Office of Youth Activities, Diocese of Arlington, VA